I0013143

Exploring Artificial Neural Networks

SHRAVAN GEERLAPALLY

AVSS LAVANYA

C VENUGOPAL

Copyright © 2025

All rights reserved.

ISBN: 9798308512684

DEDICATION

This book is dedicated to all my teachers

INDEX

1. Introduction to Artificial Neural Networks

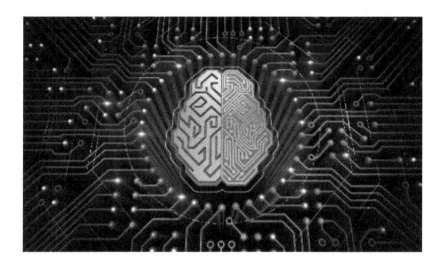

- **What Are Neural Networks?**
  - Basic definition and history of ANNs.
  - How they are inspired by the human brain.
  - Basic components: neurons, layers, weights, biases, and activation functions.
- **Why Neural Networks?**
  - Real-world applications: image recognition, language processing, game-playing AI, etc.
- **Brief History of Neural Networks**
- From early perceptrons to deep learning breakthroughs.

1 Introduction to Artificial Neural Networks

What Are Neural Networks?

Neural networks are among the most influential and transformative technologies of modern artificial intelligence (AI). These algorithms, modeled loosely after the human brain, are capable of recognizing patterns, making predictions, and even mimicking certain cognitive functions such as learning, decision-making, and perception. Neural networks have become the backbone of many real-world applications today, from healthcare diagnostics to autonomous driving, natural language processing (NLP), and computer vision.

In this section, we'll dive deeply into the definition, history, biological inspiration, and essential components of neural networks, backed by real-world examples that show how they are implemented.

Basic Definition and History of Artificial Neural Networks (ANNs)

Definition: Artificial Neural Networks (ANNs) are computational models inspired by the human brain that can learn from data, recognize patterns, and make decisions or predictions. They consist of interconnected layers of artificial neurons (also called nodes), which work together to process input data and transform it into meaningful outputs. These networks can be trained to improve their performance on specific tasks through a process of supervised learning, where they adjust their internal parameters based on feedback from known data.

History of Neural Networks

The story of neural networks began in the **1940s** with the pioneering work of scientists like Warren McCulloch and Walter Pitts. In 1943, they proposed a simple mathematical model of a neuron that could simulate logical operations such as AND, OR, and NOT. Their work laid the foundation for the study of artificial neural networks.

In **1958**, Frank Rosenblatt introduced the **perceptron**, one of the first practical neural networks. The perceptron was capable of binary classification—deciding whether an input belonged to one class or another. However, perceptrons were limited to solving only linearly separable problems (problems where two classes can be separated with a straight line).

In the **1970s**, neural network research stalled due to the inability to solve more complex problems. But in the **1980s**, with the development of **backpropagation** (a key algorithm for training multi-layer neural networks), neural networks regained attention. Backpropagation allowed the training of networks with multiple layers (known as **deep neural networks**) and solved non-linear problems, making them much more powerful.

Fast forward to the **2000s**, where advances in computational power, big data, and more sophisticated algorithms enabled the rise of **deep learning**. Deep learning refers to neural networks with many hidden layers that can model complex, non-linear relationships in large datasets. This led to breakthroughs in fields such as computer vision, language processing, and reinforcement learning.

Real-World Example:

- **Image Classification with Deep Learning**: Deep neural networks, especially **Convolutional Neural Networks (CNNs)**, are now used in real-time image recognition applications. For instance, **Google Photos** uses neural networks to recognize faces and objects in photos and categorize them, making it easier for users to search for images.

How Neural Networks Are Inspired by the Human Brain

The basic structure of artificial neural networks is inspired by the human brain, which consists of approximately 86 billion neurons. Each neuron receives electrical signals from other neurons through connections called synapses. These signals are processed by the neuron, and if they exceed a certain threshold, the neuron "fires" and transmits a signal to other connected neurons.

Key Analogies Between the Human Brain and Artificial Neural Networks:

- **Neurons**: Just as biological neurons transmit information and make decisions based on input signals, artificial neurons receive input, process it, and produce an output.
- **Synapses (Weights)**: In the brain, synapses are responsible for the strength of the connection between neurons. In artificial networks, weights represent the strength of connections between neurons, determining how much influence one neuron has on another.

- **Learning and Adaptation**: The brain learns by adjusting the strength of synapses based on experience (synaptic plasticity). Similarly, artificial neural networks learn by adjusting the weights and biases based on data and the error of previous predictions. This learning process allows neural networks to improve their performance over time.

Real-World Example:

- **Speech Recognition**: When you speak to a virtual assistant like **Apple's Siri** or **Amazon's Alexa**, neural networks process the audio signals, which are analogous to the brain's auditory processing. The network recognizes patterns in speech and learns to map audio to words. The more it "hears," the more accurately it can understand you over time, just like the human brain learns through experience.

Basic Components of Neural Networks

Artificial neural networks are composed of several core components that work together to transform inputs into outputs, and they are adjusted during the training process to improve predictions. Let's look at these components in detail:

1. Neurons (Nodes)

Each neuron in a neural network is a mathematical function that receives input, processes it, and produces output. Neurons can be visualized as small computational units that take data from the input layer, perform a mathematical operation, and pass the results to other neurons.

Function: The neuron sums its weighted inputs, applies a bias term, and then passes the result through an activation function. The activation function determines whether the neuron "fires" and contributes to the network's final output.

2. Layers of Neurons

A neural network is organized into layers:

- **Input Layer**: The input layer contains neurons that represent the features of the data. For example, in an image classification task, each pixel in the image could correspond to a neuron in the input layer.
- **Hidden Layers**: These layers are where the actual processing of the data occurs. A deep neural network can have multiple hidden layers, each learning increasingly abstract representations of the data.
- **Output Layer**: The output layer produces the final result. In a classification task, for example, the output layer might have one neuron for each possible class, and the neuron with the highest output value represents the predicted class.

3. Weights and Biases

- **Weights**: Every connection between neurons has an associated weight. The weight indicates how much influence one neuron has on another. During the training process, weights are adjusted to minimize the error in the network's predictions.
- **Biases**: Each neuron has a bias value, which allows the model to better fit the data by shifting the output of the activation function.

4. Activation Functions

Activation functions are mathematical operations applied to the output of neurons to introduce non-linearity to the network, enabling it to learn complex patterns. Some common activation functions are:

- **Sigmoid**: Used primarily in binary classification tasks, as it outputs values between 0 and 1, making it suitable for probability estimation.
- **ReLU (Rectified Linear Unit)**: Commonly used in deep networks. ReLU outputs the input if positive, otherwise it outputs zero. This function helps mitigate the vanishing gradient problem, which is common in deep networks.
- **Softmax**: Often used in the output layer for multi-class classification problems, converting raw network outputs into a probability distribution over different classes.

Real-World Example:

- **Autonomous Vehicles**: In self-driving cars, neural networks process data from sensors like cameras, radar, and LiDAR. The input layer processes the raw sensor data, hidden layers learn spatial relationships and recognize objects like pedestrians and other vehicles, and the output layer produces steering, braking, and acceleration commands to navigate the car safely.

Training a Neural Network

Training a neural network involves adjusting the weights and biases to minimize the difference between the network's predictions and the actual outcomes. This process typically involves two key steps: **forward propagation** and **backpropagation**.

1. **Forward Propagation**:
    o   The input data is passed through the network's layers, with each neuron applying its weights, biases, and activation functions to produce an output.
    o   The output layer generates a prediction, which is then compared to the true label (in supervised learning tasks).
2. **Backpropagation**:
    o   This is the core of the training process. Once the error between the predicted and actual values is calculated, the backpropagation algorithm propagates this error backward through the network.
    o   The algorithm adjusts the weights and biases using gradient descent or similar optimization techniques to minimize the error and improve the model's accuracy.

Real-World Example:

Healthcare Diagnostics: Neural networks are increasingly being used in medical fields, such as for diagnosing diseases from medical images. For example, a neural network trained on thousands of MRI images of the brain can learn to detect signs of diseases like Alzheimer's or brain tumors. During training, the network compares its predictions to the actual diagnoses (labels) and adjusts its parameters to reduce errors.

Why Neural Networks?

Neural networks have become one of the most important tools in the field of artificial intelligence (AI) due to their ability to solve complex problems that traditional algorithms struggle to handle. Their flexibility, capacity for learning, and adaptability to various types of data make them powerful models for a wide range of applications. Let's explore why neural networks are so well-suited for these tasks and how they are applied in the real world, particularly in **image recognition**, **language processing**, **game-playing AI**, and more.

Why Neural Networks Are So Powerful

Neural networks are uniquely suited to handle tasks that involve **high-dimensional data**, **non-linear relationships**, and **complex patterns**. Here's why they excel:

1. **Learning from Data**: Unlike traditional programming methods, where rules and logic are explicitly coded, neural networks learn patterns and structures from large datasets. This ability to **self-learn** from data allows neural networks to make sense of complex, unstructured inputs (e.g., images, sound, text) and use them to perform tasks.
2. **Non-linearity**: Neural networks can model **non-linear relationships**. Traditional algorithms that rely on linear assumptions often fail when the data contains intricate, non-linear patterns. Neural networks, with their multiple layers and activation functions, are capable of capturing these relationships.

3. **Flexibility**: Neural networks are incredibly versatile and can be used for various tasks, from supervised learning (where the data comes with labels) to unsupervised learning (where the system learns patterns from data without labeled outputs) and reinforcement learning (where the system learns through trial and error).
4. **Scalability**: With the advancement of deep learning, neural networks have grown to handle massive amounts of data and can scale well with increasing dataset sizes, making them ideal for modern applications that involve large-scale data.

Real-World Applications of Neural Networks

Let's explore some **real-world applications** of neural networks, highlighting their versatility and power in solving complex problems across various domains:

1. Image Recognition

One of the most prominent and widespread applications of neural networks is **image recognition**, particularly with the use of **Convolutional Neural Networks (CNNs)**. CNNs are specialized neural networks designed for analyzing visual data, making them incredibly effective in identifying objects, faces, scenes, and more.

How It Works:

- CNNs break an image into small sections and analyze different features (edges, textures, patterns) at multiple scales.
- The layers of the network process different aspects of the image, from basic shapes in earlier layers to complex objects in deeper layers.
- Finally, the output layer provides a classification or recognition result (e.g., "cat" or "dog").

- **Facial Recognition**: Neural networks are used in applications such as **Apple's Face ID** and **Facebook's photo tagging**. By learning from thousands of images, the network becomes proficient at distinguishing faces, even under varying lighting conditions, angles, or ages.
- **Medical Imaging**: Neural networks are used in healthcare to analyze X-rays, MRIs, and CT scans to identify diseases such as cancer or brain tumors. For instance, a **deep learning model** might be trained to detect lung cancer in chest X-rays with remarkable accuracy, often surpassing human experts in terms of efficiency and reliability.
- **Autonomous Vehicles**: Self-driving cars rely on image recognition to understand the environment around them. Neural networks process images from cameras and LiDAR sensors to detect pedestrians, other vehicles, road signs, and obstacles, making driving decisions in real time.

2. Language Processing (Natural Language Processing - NLP)

Neural networks, particularly **Recurrent Neural Networks (RNNs)** and **Transformers**, have made huge strides in the field of **Natural Language Processing (NLP)**. NLP is concerned with the interaction between computers and human language, enabling machines to understand, interpret, and respond to text or speech in a human-like manner.

How It Works:

- RNNs are designed to handle sequential data, like text, where the meaning of a word depends on the words that come before or after it. They process each word in the sentence and maintain a memory of previous words (i.e., context).
- Transformers, a newer model architecture, excel at handling long-range dependencies in text and can process entire sentences simultaneously, making them highly efficient for NLP tasks.

Real-World Example:

- **Google Translate**: Google's **Neural Machine Translation** system uses neural networks to translate text from one language to another. The network learns how to map phrases in one language to equivalent phrases in another, improving over time with more data.
- **Chatbots and Virtual Assistants**: Virtual assistants like **Amazon's Alexa**, **Google Assistant**, and **Apple's Siri** leverage neural networks to process natural language input and provide appropriate responses. They understand speech patterns, intent, and context, enabling them to carry out tasks like setting reminders, answering questions, and controlling smart home devices.

- **Sentiment Analysis**: Companies use neural networks for sentiment analysis to monitor customer feedback and social media conversations. By understanding the sentiment behind text (positive, negative, neutral), businesses can make informed decisions about product improvements, marketing strategies, and customer support.

3. Game-Playing AI

Neural networks have been used extensively in AI systems designed to play games. These AI systems learn to play games by simulating thousands or millions of possible game scenarios, adjusting their strategies through trial and error.

How It Works:

- Neural networks are trained on game data (e.g., past game plays, strategies, or simulated environments).
- Reinforcement learning techniques are used, where the system receives feedback on its performance and adjusts its strategies based on rewards and penalties.

Real-World Example:

- **AlphaGo**: One of the most famous examples of neural networks in game-playing is **AlphaGo**, developed by **DeepMind**. AlphaGo defeated the world champion in the ancient board game **Go** in 2016. It used a combination of neural networks and deep reinforcement learning to evaluate game positions and make strategic moves, learning from millions of games to enhance its performance.
- **Chess and Dota 2**: AI systems like **Stockfish** (for chess) and **OpenAI Five** (for Dota 2) also use neural networks to analyze vast numbers of possible moves and strategies. These systems have defeated human world champions, showcasing

the immense power of neural networks in strategic decision-making.

4. Healthcare and Diagnostics

Neural networks are rapidly transforming healthcare, particularly in diagnostic imaging, drug discovery, and personalized medicine. By analyzing medical data such as images, genetic information, and patient records, neural networks can aid in early diagnosis and the development of tailored treatment plans.

How It Works:

- Deep learning models are trained on large datasets of medical images, patient records, and other health-related data. By recognizing patterns and anomalies, these networks can detect diseases, predict patient outcomes, and assist doctors in making more accurate decisions.

Real-World Example:

- **AI in Radiology**: Companies like **Zebra Medical Vision** use neural networks to analyze X-ray, CT, and MRI scans to detect conditions such as pneumonia, breast cancer, or stroke. The AI can identify issues that might be missed by human radiologists, especially in early stages when treatment is most effective.
- **Drug Discovery**: Neural networks are also used to analyze molecular structures and predict which compounds could be effective in treating specific diseases. **Atomwise**, for instance, uses deep learning to predict how molecules will interact, speeding up the process of drug discovery and helping find potential treatments for diseases like Ebola or cancer.

5. Finance and Fraud Detection

In the finance sector, neural networks are used to detect fraudulent transactions, predict stock market trends, and optimize investment portfolios.

How It Works:

- Neural networks analyze historical transaction data, looking for patterns that could indicate fraud, such as unusual spending behavior or transactions in unexpected locations.
- For investment prediction, neural networks process market data and identify trends or anomalies that could signal an opportunity or risk.

Real-World Example:

- **Credit Card Fraud Detection**: Banks use neural networks to monitor credit card transactions in real-time. If a transaction deviates from typical patterns (such as a high-value purchase in a different country), the system flags it for further investigation, protecting customers from fraud.
- **Stock Market Prediction**: Investment firms use neural networks to analyze stock market data and predict price movements. By processing large datasets, these networks can identify patterns that help traders make more informed decisions.

Brief History of Neural Networks

The journey of neural networks has been long and eventful, spanning several decades of scientific advancements, setbacks, and breakthroughs. From the humble beginnings of the **perceptron** in the 1950s to the monumental rise of **deep learning** in the 21st century, neural networks have undergone significant evolution. Let's trace the history of neural networks, exploring key milestones, key figures, and major advancements that paved the way for today's state-of-the-art AI systems.

Early Beginnings: The Birth of Neural Networks (1940s-1950s)

The origins of neural networks can be traced back to the 1940s and 1950s, when the first ideas of artificial intelligence began to take shape. Scientists were inspired by the brain's ability to process information and make decisions and sought to replicate this process in machines.

1943 - McCulloch and Pitts Neuron Model:

- **Warren McCulloch** and **Walter Pitts** were among the first to propose a mathematical model of a neuron in 1943. This model was simple but groundbreaking, as it introduced the idea of **binary neurons** that could be activated or deactivated based on a set threshold.
- The McCulloch-Pitts neuron could perform logical operations (AND, OR, NOT), laying the foundation for further exploration into artificial neurons.
- This idea sparked early thoughts on artificial neural networks,

as McCulloch and Pitts' work demonstrated how simple units could be combined to perform more complex tasks.

1950s - The Rise of the Perceptron:

- In the late 1950s, **Frank Rosenblatt**, a psychologist, introduced the **perceptron**, one of the first neural networks capable of learning from data.
- The perceptron was a single-layer neural network that could classify inputs into two categories, making it suitable for simple tasks like distinguishing between different shapes or objects.
- The perceptron was a revolutionary step forward, as it marked the first instance where machines could learn patterns from input data without being explicitly programmed to do so.

Real-World Example:

- Early machine learning algorithms like the perceptron could be used to classify simple shapes. For instance, a perceptron might be trained to distinguish between squares and circles based on their features (such as edges and angles).

Challenges and Setbacks: The AI Winter (1960s-1970s)

Despite the early enthusiasm, the development of neural networks faced significant challenges in the following decades. Progress stalled in part due to limitations in both technology and understanding.

1969 - Minsky and Papert's "Perceptrons" Book:

- **Marvin Minsky** and **Seymour Papert** published a critical book in 1969 titled **"Perceptrons"**, which highlighted the limitations of single-layer perceptrons. They demonstrated that perceptrons could only solve linearly separable problems (i.e., problems that could be separated by a straight line), but not more complex tasks like XOR (exclusive OR), a simple logical operation.
- This criticism led to a decrease in interest and investment in neural networks, contributing to a period known as the **AI Winter**, where funding and research into AI-related fields, including neural networks, sharply declined.

Setback in Research:

- During this time, many researchers abandoned neural networks in favor of more traditional symbolic AI approaches, where rules and logic were explicitly coded. While symbolic AI made advances in specific applications (like expert systems), the neural network approach was largely put on hold.

Revival and the Emergence of Backpropagation (1980s)

The 1980s saw a major resurgence in neural network research, thanks to a series of breakthroughs, the most important of which was the development of the **backpropagation algorithm**.

1986 - Backpropagation Algorithm:

- **Geoffrey Hinton, David Rumelhart**, and **Ronald J. Williams** are credited with rediscovering and popularizing the **backpropagation algorithm** in 1986. This algorithm provided an efficient way to train multi-layer networks, also known as **deep neural networks**.
- **Backpropagation** works by calculating the error in the network's predictions, then propagating that error back through the network to adjust the weights and biases of neurons in order to minimize the error. This made it feasible to train networks with more than one layer, overcoming the limitations of early perceptrons and allowing neural networks to solve much more complex, non-linear problems.

1980s - Multi-Layer Perceptrons (MLPs):

- With backpropagation, researchers were able to build **multi-layer perceptrons (MLPs)**, which consisted of multiple layers of neurons. These networks could learn much more complex patterns and solve a broader range of problems, such as speech recognition, image classification, and more.
- Although still limited by computational resources, this period marked the return of neural networks as a viable tool for machine learning and AI research.

Real-World Example:

- During the 1980s, early neural networks began to be applied to tasks like speech recognition. For example, **HTK (Hidden Markov Model Toolkit)** was developed to improve speech recognition systems by using neural networks to better handle the variations in human speech.

Deep Learning and the Explosion of Neural Networks (2000s-Present)

While the 1980s and 1990s revived interest in neural networks, it wasn't until the 2000s that **deep learning** emerged as the dominant paradigm for machine learning, thanks to advances in computing power, the availability of large datasets, and more sophisticated algorithms.

2006 - The Birth of Deep Learning:

- **Geoffrey Hinton** and his colleagues published a groundbreaking paper in 2006 on **deep belief networks** (DBNs), a type of deep neural network that could learn hierarchical features from data.
- This work is considered one of the seminal moments in the rise of **deep learning**—a subfield of machine learning focused on training deep (multi-layer) neural networks. These networks could learn increasingly abstract representations of data, making them ideal for tasks like image and speech recognition.
- With the advent of **graphics processing units (GPUs)**, which could accelerate the training process, deep learning models became much more computationally feasible, opening the door for larger, more complex neural networks to be trained on vast datasets.

2012 - AlexNet and ImageNet Breakthrough:

- In 2012, a deep neural network called **AlexNet**, developed by **Alex Krizhevsky, Ilya Sutskever**, and **Geoffrey Hinton**, won the **ImageNet competition** by a wide margin, achieving a significant reduction in error rates for image classification tasks.
- AlexNet used a **Convolutional Neural Network (CNN)**, which was specifically designed to process and classify images. It was trained on GPUs, enabling it to handle large-scale datasets and achieve results that were previously unimaginable.
- This breakthrough is often cited as the turning point for the field of **computer vision** and deep learning, as it demonstrated the immense potential of neural networks for solving complex problems.

Real-World Example:

- **Google Photos**: Using deep learning models like CNNs, **Google Photos** automatically categorizes images, recognizes faces, and allows users to search for photos using natural language queries (e.g., "beach," "birthday party"). This is possible because of advancements in deep learning, which allows the system to identify and tag objects and scenes within images accurately.

2014-2015 - Generative Models and Reinforcement Learning:

- The field expanded further with the introduction of **Generative Adversarial Networks (GANs)** by **Ian Goodfellow** and the rise of **reinforcement learning** models, particularly through projects like **AlphaGo** and **Deep Q-Networks (DQN)**.
- **GANs** enabled the generation of new, realistic data (images, text, music) by training two neural networks in opposition, creating an output that is indistinguishable from real data.
- **AlphaGo**, developed by **DeepMind**, used deep neural networks and reinforcement learning to defeat world champions in the game of **Go**—a monumental achievement that demonstrated the potential of neural networks in strategic decision-making.

Present Day and Future Directions

As we enter the 2020s, deep learning and neural networks continue to evolve. New architectures and innovations are expanding their capabilities:

- **Transformers**, used in language models like **GPT** and **BERT**, have revolutionized natural language processing.
- **Self-supervised learning** and **unsupervised learning** methods are gaining traction, enabling neural networks to learn from unlabeled data, a massive leap forward in overcoming the dependence on labeled datasets.
- **Neural networks in robotics**, **artificial creativity**, and **multi-modal systems** are pushing the boundaries of what is possible.

Real-World Example:

- **GPT-3**: OpenAI's **GPT-3** (Generative Pretrained Transformer) is a deep learning model that can generate human-like text based on a given prompt. It can write essays, answer questions, and even generate computer code. This model is the result of years of research and advancements in neural networks and natural language processing.

Mathematical Foundations

- **Linear Algebra**
  - o Vectors, matrices, and operations used in ANNs.
- **Calculus**
  - o Derivatives, gradients, and optimization.
- **Probability and Statistics**
  - o Basics for understanding loss functions and error minimization.
- **Optimization Techniques-**Gradient descent, stochastic gradient descent (SGD), and advanced optimizers.

Mathematical Foundations of Neural Networks: Linear Algebra

To truly understand how neural networks work, one must delve into the core **mathematical foundations** that underpin the operations and learning algorithms that drive them. One of the most critical areas of mathematics in neural networks is **linear algebra**. Linear algebra provides the tools necessary to manipulate the data and parameters that flow through artificial neural networks (ANNs), especially in terms of the **vectors** and **matrices** that are central to the computations.

Let's take a closer look at the key linear algebra concepts that form the backbone of ANNs, focusing on **vectors**, **matrices**, and the essential operations used to train and evaluate neural networks.

Vectors: The Building Blocks of Neural Networks

At the most fundamental level, **vectors** are an essential building block in neural networks. In mathematics, a vector is a quantity defined by both a magnitude and direction, and it can be visualized as an ordered array of numbers. In the context of neural networks, vectors represent data or parameters.

What Is a Vector?

A **vector** is simply a list or an array of numbers, often used to represent points or directions in a multi-dimensional space. For example, in a neural network, each input or feature might be represented by a vector.

- **Example**: Suppose we have a simple data point representing an image. This data point can be broken down into a vector where each component represents a pixel's intensity (brightness or color value). For a grayscale image, the vector could look like this:

$$\mathbf{x} = \begin{bmatrix} 0.1 \\ 0.3 \\ 0.5 \\ 0.7 \end{bmatrix}$$

- This represents a data point (an image, in this case) as a column vector.

How Vectors Are Used in Neural Networks:

- **Input Vectors**: The **input layer** of a neural network accepts the data in the form of vectors. These vectors are then processed layer by layer.
- **Weight Vectors**: Each neuron in the network has associated weights, which are also represented as vectors. These weights define the importance of each input feature and are adjusted during training.

Vector Operations in Neural Networks:

- **Dot Product**: One of the fundamental operations with vectors in neural networks is the **dot product**, which measures how much one vector influences another. It's used in the computation of **weighted sums** in each neuron.

$$\mathbf{a} \cdot \mathbf{b} = a_1 b_1 + a_2 b_2 + \cdots + a_n b_n$$

This operation is key in the calculation of the activations in a neuron.

- **Norm (Magnitude)**: The norm of a vector is a measure of its length or size, commonly used for tasks like **regularization** or ensuring stability during training.

$$\|\mathbf{x}\| = \sqrt{x_1^2 + x_2^2 + \cdots + x_n^2}$$

- **Vector Addition and Scalar Multiplication**: These operations are used to update the inputs and weights in neural networks. When training a neural network, adjustments to the weights are made based on **gradients**, which involve vector addition and scaling.

Matrices: Structuring Data and Parameters

While vectors are one-dimensional arrays, **matrices** are two-dimensional arrays of numbers. In neural networks, matrices are used extensively to represent and manipulate **datasets, weight parameters**, and **activations** of neurons across layers.

What Is a Matrix?

A **matrix** is a two-dimensional array of numbers arranged in rows and columns. In the context of ANNs, matrices are used to represent collections of data points, weight parameters, and transformations applied to data as it moves through the network layers.

- **Example**: A **matrix** could represent the weights between an input layer and a hidden layer in a neural network. If the input layer has 3 nodes and the hidden layer has 4, the weight matrix W would have a shape of 4×34 times 34×3, with 4 rows (one for each neuron in the hidden layer) and 3 columns (one for each input feature).

$$W = \begin{bmatrix} w_{11} & w_{12} & w_{13} \\ w_{21} & w_{22} & w_{23} \\ w_{31} & w_{32} & w_{33} \\ w_{41} & w_{42} & w_{43} \end{bmatrix}$$

How Matrices Are Used in Neural Networks:

- **Weight Matrices**: Neural networks consist of layers, and each layer has a set of weights that control how the input data is transformed. These weights are stored in matrices and multiplied by the input vectors to compute the output of each layer.
- **Layer Transformation**:

  The operation $z = W \cdot x + b$

  $z = W \cdot x + b$ represents a layer transformation, where:

  - z is the output of the layer.
  - W is the weight matrix.
  - x is the input vector.
  - b is the bias vector.

- **Input Data**: The input data itself is often represented as a **matrix**. For example, if you have a dataset with 100 data points, each containing 5 features, this dataset would be represented as a 100×5100 times 5100×5 matrix, where each row is a vector representing a single data point.
- **Batch Processing**: Neural networks often process multiple data points at once using **batch processing**. This is where matrices truly shine because operations can be done on the entire dataset at once. Instead of processing each input vector individually, you can represent the entire batch of inputs as a matrix and perform matrix multiplications efficiently.

Matrix Operations in Neural Networks:

- **Matrix Multiplication**: One of the most important matrix operations is **matrix multiplication**. When the weight matrix W is multiplied by the input vector x, the result is a new vector z representing the weighted sum of inputs for each neuron in the next layer:

  $z = W \cdot x$

  This operation is repeated for each layer in the neural network.

- **Matrix Addition**: After multiplying the weight matrix by the input, we usually add a **bias vector** b to the result to shift the activation, enabling the network to model more complex functions.

Operations in Neural Networks: Applying Linear Algebra

Now that we have discussed vectors and matrices, let's dive deeper into how these operations come together in the process of training and operating a neural network.

Forward Propagation:

In a typical feedforward neural network, the forward propagation process involves passing data through the layers of the network. This process can be represented using vector and matrix operations.

- For an input vector x, the first layer computes the output as:

$$\mathbf{z_1} = W_1 \cdot \mathbf{x} + \mathbf{b_1}$$

- Then, an activation function f is applied to z to obtain the output of the layer:

$$\mathbf{a_1} = f(\mathbf{z_1})$$

- The process is repeated for each subsequent layer, with the output of each layer feeding into the next one.

Backpropagation:

During training, neural networks adjust their weights using a process called **backpropagation**, which involves updating the weights based on the gradient of the error with respect to the weights.

- **Gradient Computation**: The gradient (or slope) of the error with respect to the weights can be computed using **partial derivatives**. This allows the network to make small adjustments to the weights, reducing the error and improving predictions over time.

- **Weight Updates**: The weights are updated using the **gradient descent algorithm**. For a given weight www, the update rule is:

$$w := w - \eta \cdot \frac{\partial E}{\partial w}$$

where η is the learning rate, and $\frac{\partial E}{\partial w}$ is the partial derivative of the error E with respect to the weight w. These calculations involve the use of both vectors and matrices to propagate the error backward through the network.

Conclusion: Linear Algebra's Role in Neural Networks

In neural networks, **linear algebra** plays an indispensable role in organizing and transforming data as it flows through layers of neurons. The operations on **vectors** and **matrices** enable the network to process and adjust weights efficiently during both forward and backward passes. Understanding these mathematical tools is crucial for anyone looking to dive deep into the workings of ANNs and neural network training.

- **Vectors** allow us to represent data and parameters succinctly.
- **Matrices** enable the handling of large datasets and complex transformations between layers of the network.
- Matrix and vector operations, such as multiplication, addition, and dot products, form the core of **forward propagation** and **backpropagation** processes.

As neural networks become deeper and more complex, the importance of linear algebra grows, as it provides the foundation for the efficient computation and optimization of large-scale models.

Mathematical Foundations of Neural Networks: Calculus, Probability & Statistics, and Optimization Techniques

In the development and training of neural networks, several core mathematical concepts come into play, most notably **calculus**, **probability and statistics**, and **optimization techniques**. These fields of mathematics provide the tools needed to adjust the parameters of the model, minimize errors, and achieve the desired outputs. Let's break down these areas in detail to understand how they contribute to neural networks.

1. Calculus: Derivatives, Gradients, and Optimization

Derivatives and Their Importance in Neural Networks

Calculus, specifically the concept of **derivatives**, plays a central role in the optimization process during the training of neural networks. In the context of neural networks, the goal is to adjust the model's parameters (such as weights and biases) so that the network's output matches the expected output. This adjustment process requires the calculation of the rate at which the error changes with respect to the parameters, which is where **derivatives** come into play.

A **derivative** measures how a function changes as its input changes. In the case of neural networks, the "function" is the **loss function**, which quantifies the error or difference between the predicted output and the actual output. By computing derivatives, we can determine the direction in which the loss function increases or decreases, enabling the model to adjust its parameters accordingly.

Gradient and Gradient Descent

- The **gradient** is a vector of partial derivatives that describes the rate of change of the loss function with respect to each parameter (weight and bias). Essentially, it tells us in which direction to adjust the parameters to minimize the error. The gradient points to the steepest ascent of the loss function, and by following the negative gradient, we can move in the direction that reduces the error.
- The process of adjusting the parameters to minimize the loss function is called **gradient descent**. In simple terms, **gradient descent** is an iterative optimization algorithm used to minimize the loss by adjusting weights and biases in small steps proportional to the gradient at each step.

The Optimization Process:

The goal is to minimize the loss function L with respect to the model's parameters θ, which can include weights W and biases b. The update rule for gradient descent can be expressed as:

$$\theta \leftarrow \theta - \eta \cdot \nabla_\theta L$$

Where:

- θ represents the parameters (weights and biases).
- η is the **learning rate**, a hyperparameter that controls how large each step is.

- $\nabla\theta L$ is the gradient of the loss function with respect to the parameters, i.e., the derivative.

Through repeated application of this update rule, the neural network gradually moves towards the optimal set of parameters that minimizes the loss.

Real-World Example:

In image classification, for example, the neural network's weights are adjusted so that the network produces the correct label for each image. By computing the gradient of the loss with respect to the weights and biases, the network can learn to make better predictions, refining its parameters through multiple iterations until it converges to a solution with minimal error.

2. Probability and Statistics: Basics for Understanding Loss Functions and Error Minimization

Probability and statistics are crucial in understanding how neural networks deal with uncertainty and variation in data. Neural networks are often used in **predictive modeling** and classification tasks, where the goal is to predict the most likely outcome or category given an input. In these contexts, probability and statistics help in designing the **loss functions**, which guide the network to learn effectively from the data.

Loss Functions and Error Minimization

- A **loss function** (or cost function) quantifies the difference between the predicted output and the actual output. The objective of training a neural network is to **minimize** this loss. Common loss functions include:
  - **Mean Squared Error (MSE)**: Used for regression tasks where the goal is to predict a continuous value.

$$L = \frac{1}{N} \sum_{i=1}^{N} (y_i - \hat{y}_i)^2$$

Where yi is the actual value, y^i is the predicted value, and N is the number of data points.

- ○ **Cross-Entropy Loss**: Used for classification tasks where the output is a probability distribution over classes. It is derived from **information theory** and measures the difference between two probability distributions (the predicted and the true distribution).

$$L = - \sum_{i=1}^{C} y_i \log(\hat{y}_i)$$

Where C is the number of classes, yi is the true label (0 or 1), and y_i is the predicted probability for the class.

Bayesian Probability:

In many cases, neural networks rely on **Bayesian methods** to manage uncertainty in predictions. **Bayes' theorem** is used to update the probability of a hypothesis as more data is available. In neural networks, this is especially important in **probabilistic modeling**, where predictions are made in terms of probability distributions.

Real-World Example:

Consider a neural network trained to recognize cats in images. The network might output a probability score for whether an image contains a cat. The loss function (e.g., **cross-entropy loss**) will calculate the difference between the predicted probability and the actual label (cat or no cat). The neural network's parameters will be adjusted to minimize this loss function, effectively reducing the error in the network's predictions.

3. Optimization Techniques: Gradient Descent, Stochastic Gradient Descent (SGD), and Advanced Optimizers

The optimization process in neural networks relies on adjusting the parameters (weights and biases) to minimize the loss function. The most common technique used to do this is **gradient descent**. However, there are various optimizations and refinements that make gradient descent more effective, especially for large and complex networks.

Gradient Descent: The Basics

Gradient descent is a fundamental optimization algorithm used to minimize the loss function. It works by updating the parameters in the opposite direction of the gradient to reduce the error iteratively.

The general update rule is:

$$\theta_t = \theta_{t-1} - \eta \cdot \nabla_\theta L(\theta_{t-1})$$

Where:

- θ_t are the parameters at iteration t.
- η is the learning rate (step size).
- $\nabla_\theta L$ is the gradient of the loss with respect to the parameters.

Stochastic Gradient Descent (SGD)

Stochastic Gradient Descent (SGD) is a variant of gradient descent where instead of using the entire dataset to compute the gradient at each step (which can be computationally expensive), we compute the gradient using a single randomly chosen training example (or a small batch). This makes the algorithm faster and more scalable for large datasets.

The update rule in **SGD** is:

$$\theta_t = \theta_{t-1} - \eta \cdot \nabla_\theta L(\theta_{t-1}; x_i, y_i)$$

Where:

- (x_i, y_i) is the random training example.
- $L(\theta_{t-1}; x_i, y_i)$ is the loss computed using that training example.

While SGD can converge more quickly than standard gradient descent, it tends to be more noisy, meaning the parameter updates can fluctuate significantly from one step to the next. This is where more advanced optimizers come into play.

Advanced Optimizers:

To address the limitations of vanilla gradient descent and SGD, several **advanced optimization algorithms** have been developed, such as:

- **Momentum**: Momentum helps smooth out the updates by considering past gradients, allowing the algorithm to build up speed in directions where the gradient consistently points. This can speed up convergence and reduce oscillations.

  $$v_t = \beta v_{t-1} + (1 - \beta)\nabla_\theta L$$

  Where v_t is the velocity (or accumulated gradient) at time step t

  Beta β is a hyperparameter controlling the momentum.

- **AdaGrad**: AdaGrad adapts the learning rate for each parameter based on the historical gradients, scaling down the learning rate for parameters that have already seen large gradients and scaling up the learning rate for parameters that have seen small gradients.
- **RMSprop**: RMSprop (Root Mean Squared Propagation) modifies AdaGrad by considering a moving average of the squared gradients. This helps solve the problem of the learning rate shrinking too quickly.
- **Adam**: Adam (Adaptive Moment Estimation) combines ideas from momentum and RMSprop. It computes adaptive learning rates for each parameter by considering both the first moment (mean) and second moment (uncentered variance) of the gradients. Adam has become one of the most popular optimizers due to its robustness and efficiency.

The Adam update rule is:

$$m_t = \beta_1 m_{t-1} + (1 - \beta_1)\nabla_\theta L$$

$$v_t = \beta_2 v_{t-1} + (1 - \beta_2)\nabla_\theta L^2$$

$$\hat{m}_t = \frac{m_t}{1 - \beta_1^t}, \quad \hat{v}_t = \frac{v_t}{1 - \beta_2^t}$$

$$\theta_t = \theta_{t-1} - \eta \cdot \frac{\hat{m}_t}{\sqrt{\hat{v}_t} + \epsilon}$$

Real-World Example:

Imagine training a deep neural network for a large-scale image classification task. If you use **SGD**, each training step may be noisy and take a long time to converge. By using **Adam** or **RMSprop**, the optimization process becomes more stable and converges faster, leading to better model performance in less time.

Anatomy of a Neural Network

- **Neurons and Layers**
  - Details of the artificial neuron model (input, weights, summation, activation function).
  - Different types of layers: input, hidden, and output layers.
- **Activation Functions**
  - Sigmoid, ReLU, tanh, and other activation functions.
- **Feedforward Networks**
  - How information flows through a network.
- **Backpropagation-** Training neural networks using the backpropagation algorithm

Anatomy of a Neural Network

The anatomy of a neural network encompasses various components that work in harmony to process input data, learn from it, and produce useful outputs. Understanding these components in greater detail is crucial for grasping how neural networks function and how they can be applied to a range of problems. In this chapter, we will dive deeper into the **neurons and layers**, **activation functions**, **feedforward networks**, and **backpropagation**, explaining each element's significance and their interactions within the network.

1. Neurons and Layers

At the heart of a neural network lies the **artificial neuron**—the basic computational unit that mimics the function of biological neurons. While the biological neuron transmits electrical signals, an artificial neuron processes numerical data through a series of operations, including weighted sums and activation functions.

The Artificial Neuron Model

An artificial neuron operates on the following key elements:

1. **Inputs**: These are the data values fed into the neuron. In a neural network, the inputs can be raw data (such as pixel values in an image, or sensor readings) or outputs from the previous layer of neurons.
   - For example, in an image classification problem, each input could represent a pixel or a small group of pixels from an image.
2. **Weights**: Each input is associated with a **weight** that determines the strength or importance of that input in the computation. The weights allow the network to adjust and

learn the relationships between inputs and outputs during the training phase. Higher weights signify that an input is more influential, while lower weights mean less influence.

- o Initially, weights are usually set randomly but are updated during training to improve the model's performance.

3. **Summation**: The neuron computes a **weighted sum** of the inputs. Mathematically, this is represented as:

$$z = \sum_{i=1}^{n} x_i \cdot w_i + b$$

Where:

- o x_i are the input values,
- o w_i are the corresponding weights,
- o b is the **bias** term (discussed below).

The **bias** term is an additional parameter that helps shift the activation function's output. The bias allows the neuron to make decisions even when all inputs are zero, contributing to the flexibility of the network.

4. **Activation Function**: After the summation, the result is passed through an **activation function** that determines the output of the neuron. The activation function introduces **non-linearity** into the model, enabling it to learn complex patterns in the data. Without non-linearity, even deep networks would reduce to simple linear models, making them incapable of handling intricate data.

Types of Layers in a Neural Network

Neural networks consist of multiple **layers**, each responsible for different stages of computation. The most common types of layers include:

1. **Input Layer**:
   - The input layer is where data enters the neural network. In an image recognition task, this layer might consist of one neuron for each pixel in the image. For structured data (like tabular data), the input layer consists of one neuron per feature.
   - The neurons in the input layer simply pass the data on to the subsequent layers without modification.
2. **Hidden Layers**:
   - Hidden layers are intermediate layers between the input and output layers. These layers perform more complex computations, transforming the raw data into more abstract representations.
   - **Deep neural networks** have multiple hidden layers, allowing the network to learn progressively more complex features at each layer. For example, in image classification, the first hidden layer might detect simple features like edges, the next layer might detect shapes, and later layers could recognize specific objects.
   - Neurons in hidden layers perform operations such as weighted sums and apply activation functions to transform the data as it moves through the network.

3. **Output Layer**:
   - The output layer produces the final result or prediction of the neural network. In a classification problem, each neuron in the output layer corresponds to one class. The output neurons may use the **softmax activation function** to output probabilities, where the sum of all probabilities is equal to 1.
   - In a regression problem, the output layer typically contains a single neuron with a linear activation function to produce continuous values.

2. Activation Functions

Activation functions play a pivotal role in introducing non-linearity to the network, which enables it to learn from complex data. Different activation functions are used depending on the problem being solved and the behavior desired from the network. Below are some of the most commonly used activation functions:

Sigmoid Activation Function

The **sigmoid** function outputs values between 0 and 1, making it useful for problems where we need to interpret outputs as probabilities, such as binary classification.

The function is given by:

$$\sigma(x) = \frac{1}{1 + e^{-x}}$$

Where:

- e^{-x} is the exponential function.

However, the sigmoid function suffers from **vanishing gradients** when its inputs become very large or very small. In these regions, the gradient (used during backpropagation) becomes extremely small, slowing down learning.

ReLU (Rectified Linear Unit)

ReLU is one of the most widely used activation functions due to its simplicity and efficiency. It outputs the input directly if it's positive; otherwise, it outputs zero.

ReLU is defined as:

$$\text{ReLU}(x) = \max(0, x)$$

Where:

- If $x>0$, the output is x,
- If $x\leq0$, the output is 0.

- **Advantages of ReLU:**
  - ○ It allows the network to model more complex, non-linear relationships.
  - ○ It helps mitigate the vanishing gradient problem, which allows faster learning in deep networks.

- **Drawbacks of ReLU:**
  - ○ ReLU can cause **dead neurons**, where neurons stop activating altogether and effectively "die." This occurs when the neuron's input is always negative, causing its output to be zero.

Tanh (Hyperbolic Tangent)

The **tanh** function is similar to the sigmoid function but maps the output to a range between -1 and 1, rather than between 0 and 1.

The function is given by:

$$\tanh(x) = \frac{e^x - e^{-x}}{e^x + e^{-x}}$$

- **Advantages:**
  - ○ Because it's centered around 0, tanh typically performs better than sigmoid, as it avoids outputting the same value for both large positive and negative inputs.

- **Drawbacks**:
  - o Like sigmoid, it suffers from the **vanishing gradient problem**, though less severely.

Softmax

The **softmax** function is typically used in the output layer of neural networks for multi-class classification problems. It converts the raw output values (logits) from the network into probabilities by exponentiating and normalizing them. The output of the softmax function for each class will be a value between 0 and 1, with the sum of all outputs equal to 1.

Mathematically, for class kkk, the softmax function is given by:

$$\text{softmax}(z_k) = \frac{e^{z_k}}{\sum_{j=1}^{K} e^{z_j}}$$

Where:

- z_k is the raw output (logit) for class k,
- K is the total number of classes.

3. Feedforward Networks

In a **feedforward neural network**, data moves in one direction— from the input layer through the hidden layers to the output layer. This is the simplest and most common type of neural network, where each layer of neurons only communicates with the subsequent layer.

How Information Flows Through the Network

The flow of information in a feedforward neural network is as follows:

1. **Input Layer**: Data is fed into the input layer, where each feature of the data is represented by a neuron. These values are then passed on to the neurons in the next layer.
2. **Hidden Layers**: In each hidden layer, the inputs are processed by the neurons, which perform computations on them. Each neuron computes a weighted sum of its inputs and applies an activation function to produce its output. This output is then passed to the next layer of neurons.
3. **Output Layer**: The output layer takes the data from the final hidden layer, processes it, and produces the final prediction. In a classification task, the output layer typically uses the softmax function to produce class probabilities. In regression tasks, the output layer might use a linear activation function to produce continuous predictions.

Real-World Example:

Consider a neural network trained to recognize images of animals. The network takes in an image as input, processes the image in the hidden layers (which may learn to detect edges, shapes, and objects), and outputs probabilities for each class (e.g., cat, dog, horse) in the output layer. By iteratively refining the weights through training, the network becomes better at identifying animals.

4. Backpropagation: Training Neural Networks

Backpropagation is the algorithm that allows neural networks to learn from their mistakes and improve their predictions over time. This is done by calculating the **gradient of the loss function** (which measures how far the network's predictions are from the actual values) and updating the model's weights to reduce this error.

How Backpropagation Works

1. **Forward Pass**: During the forward pass, the input data is passed through the network, and an output is generated. The output is then compared to the true label using a **loss function**, such as cross-entropy for classification or mean squared error for regression.

2. **Loss Calculation**: The loss function measures how well the network's output matches the expected result. A high loss indicates poor performance, while a low loss indicates better performance.

3. **Backward Pass**: In the backward pass, backpropagation computes the **gradient** of the loss with respect to each weight by applying the **chain rule** of calculus. This process determines how much each weight in the network contributed to the loss.
   o For each weight, we calculate how changing it would affect the loss, then use this information to adjust the weights.

4. **Weight Update**: The network's weights are updated using an optimization algorithm like **gradient descent**. Weights are adjusted by moving in the opposite direction of the gradient, reducing the loss.
   o The weight update rule is given by:

$$w := w - \eta \cdot \frac{\partial L}{\partial w}$$

Where η is the learning rate, and $\partial L/\partial w$ is the gradient of the loss with respect to the weight.

5. **Iterative Process**: The forward pass, loss calculation, backward pass, and weight updates are repeated for many iterations (or epochs). As the network sees more data and adjusts its weights, it learns to make more accurate predictions.

Real-World Example:

When training a neural network to predict the price of a house based on features like square footage, number of bedrooms, and location, backpropagation ensures that the network improves its predictions over time. After each iteration, the weights are adjusted based on the error, helping the model gradually minimize the difference between predicted and actual house prices.

Types of Neural Networks

The realm of neural networks is vast, with numerous architectures developed to solve different types of problems. Each neural network type is built with a specific structure and design to address challenges unique to particular domains. This chapter delves into several foundational and advanced types of neural networks, including **Feedforward Neural Networks (FNNs), Convolutional Neural Networks (CNNs), Recurrent Neural Networks (RNNs), Generative Adversarial Networks (GANs)**, and **other specialized networks** like **Radial Basis Function (RBF) Networks** and **Long Short-Term Memory (LSTM) Networks**. Understanding these network architectures will allow you to appreciate their capabilities and apply them to real-world problems in artificial intelligence and machine learning.

1. Feedforward Neural Networks (FNN)

Feedforward Neural Networks (FNNs) are the simplest type of artificial neural network and form the backbone of more complex architectures. The key feature of an FNN is that the information flows only in one direction, from the input layer through hidden layers to the output layer, with no feedback loops or cycles.

How Feedforward Neural Networks Work

- **Input Layer**: The input layer consists of neurons that correspond to the features of the data. Each feature of the data is fed into the input layer as a separate neuron, where it will be processed through the network.
- **Hidden Layers**: Hidden layers perform the actual processing. Neurons in these layers apply a weighted sum to their inputs, and an activation function is used to introduce non-linearity. The deeper the network (i.e., more hidden layers), the more abstract the features it can learn, making FNNs capable of solving complex problems.
- **Output Layer**: The output layer produces the final prediction or decision. In the case of a classification problem, the output layer typically uses a **softmax** function (for multi-class classification) to produce class probabilities. For regression, a linear activation function might be used to predict continuous values.

Applications of Feedforward Neural Networks

FNNs are foundational models that can be used across a variety of tasks, including:

- **Classification**: FNNs can classify images, texts, or signals. For example, classifying emails as spam or not, or identifying handwritten digits.

- **Regression**: FNNs can predict continuous values, such as predicting house prices, stock prices, or demand forecasting.

While FNNs are versatile, they have limitations when it comes to tasks where temporal or spatial relationships in data matter, such as time-series analysis or image recognition. These limitations led to the development of more specialized neural network architectures like CNNs and RNNs.

2. Convolutional Neural Networks (CNNs)

Convolutional Neural Networks (CNNs) are designed specifically to handle data that comes in the form of grids—such as images or videos—where spatial relationships are key to understanding the data. CNNs have become the go-to architecture for image-related tasks due to their ability to automatically learn hierarchical spatial features.

How Convolutional Neural Networks Work

The architecture of a CNN typically consists of the following layers:

- **Convolutional Layer**: This layer is the core of CNNs. It uses filters (also known as kernels) that slide across the input data (e.g., an image) and apply a **convolution operation**. The result is a **feature map** that highlights the presence of features like edges, textures, or shapes in the image. Each filter is trained to recognize specific patterns, and multiple filters are used in parallel to detect a variety of features.
  - Example: In an image classification task, one filter may detect horizontal edges, another may detect vertical edges, and another might capture color contrasts.
- **Activation Function (ReLU)**: After each convolution operation, the feature map passes through an **activation function** (typically **ReLU**), which introduces non-linearity, allowing the network to learn more complex patterns.

- **Pooling Layer**: The pooling layer reduces the spatial dimensions of the feature maps, making the network computationally efficient and helping to prevent overfitting.

- **Max pooling** is commonly used, where only the maximum value in a certain region of the feature map is retained, thus reducing the size while keeping the most important features.
- **Fully Connected Layers**: After several convolutional and pooling layers, the final feature maps are passed through one or more fully connected layers, which serve to classify the data or make predictions. This is similar to the layers of a traditional feedforward neural network.
- **Output Layer**: The output layer produces the final decision. In image classification, this could be a softmax function for multi-class problems or a sigmoid function for binary classification.

Applications of Convolutional Neural Networks

CNNs have revolutionized the field of computer vision, with applications spanning multiple industries:

- **Image Recognition and Classification**: Identifying objects or people in images (e.g., facial recognition, vehicle detection).
- **Object Detection**: Locating and identifying multiple objects within an image (e.g., self-driving car systems, surveillance).
- **Semantic Segmentation**: Assigning a class to each pixel in an image, which is critical for tasks like medical image analysis or autonomous driving.
- **Video Processing**: CNNs can be extended to process video frames, making them ideal for tasks like action recognition and video summarization.

Due to their ability to learn spatial hierarchies and their efficient training, CNNs have become the dominant architecture for image-related tasks.

3. Recurrent Neural Networks (RNNs)

Recurrent Neural Networks (RNNs) are designed for sequential data—data where the order of information is important. RNNs differ from feedforward networks in that they have **recurring connections** that allow information to flow in loops, effectively enabling the network to "remember" previous inputs. This makes them ideal for tasks where context from earlier inputs is needed to make accurate predictions.

How Recurrent Neural Networks Work

- **Sequential Processing**: At each time step, an RNN takes an input along with the hidden state (memory) from the previous time step. The hidden state is updated based on the current input and the previous hidden state, allowing the network to capture the sequential nature of the data.
- **Hidden States**: The key feature of an RNN is its ability to maintain hidden states that store information about previous time steps. This hidden state allows RNNs to make predictions that depend on past inputs.
- **Backpropagation Through Time (BPTT)**: The training of RNNs is done using **Backpropagation Through Time (BPTT)**, a technique that adjusts the weights of the network based on the error in the output, taking into account the time dependencies in the data.

Applications of Recurrent Neural Networks

RNNs are well-suited to tasks involving sequential data. Some of their primary applications include:

- **Time-Series Forecasting**: Predicting future values based on historical data. Examples include predicting stock prices, weather patterns, or energy consumption.
- **Natural Language Processing (NLP)**: RNNs are commonly used for tasks like **language modeling**, **speech recognition**, and **machine translation**. In these cases, the order of words or sounds is critical.
- **Speech Generation and Recognition**: RNNs can model the temporal dependencies in speech, enabling them to generate speech from text or transcribe audio to text.
- **Sequence Prediction**: In any domain that involves predicting sequences (e.g., predicting the next word in a sentence, generating captions for images), RNNs can effectively model these dependencies.

However, traditional RNNs have difficulty learning long-range dependencies due to the **vanishing gradient problem**. This has led to the development of more advanced variants like **LSTM** (Long Short-Term Memory) networks and **GRUs** (Gated Recurrent Units).

4. Generative Adversarial Networks (GANs)

Generative Adversarial Networks (GANs) represent a novel approach to neural network design, where two networks (a **generator** and a **discriminator**) are trained in competition with each other. The generator creates synthetic data (e.g., images), and the discriminator evaluates the authenticity of this data against real data.

How GANs Work

- **Generator Network**: The generator starts with random noise and attempts to produce data that resembles the real dataset. Over time, it learns to generate more realistic outputs by improving its understanding of the data distribution.
- **Discriminator Network**: The discriminator evaluates the authenticity of the data by distinguishing between real data from the training set and fake data generated by the generator. It outputs a probability that the input data is real.
- **Adversarial Training**: The generator and discriminator compete with each other. As the discriminator gets better at identifying fake data, the generator improves its ability to generate more realistic data. This adversarial process continues until the generator produces data that is indistinguishable from real data.

Applications of Generative Adversarial Networks

GANs have become a game-changer in fields requiring data generation and enhancement:

- **Image Generation**: GANs can generate realistic images from random noise, such as creating faces of people who don't exist or generating art.
- **Image-to-Image Translation**: GANs can transform one type of image into another. For example, turning sketches into realistic images or converting black-and-white images into color.

- **Data Augmentation**: GANs can generate additional training data when real-world data is scarce, which can be particularly useful for training deep learning models with limited data.
- **Deepfakes**: GANs have been used to create **deepfake** videos, where the faces of people in videos can be swapped convincingly.

Despite their remarkable ability to generate new data, GANs come with challenges like instability during training and the risk of producing nonsensical results.

5. Other Specialized Neural Networks

In addition to the popular neural network types mentioned above, there are several other specialized architectures that address specific challenges in machine learning. These networks provide more flexibility and power in solving specific tasks.

Radial Basis Function (RBF) Networks

RBF networks are a type of neural network used primarily for function approximation and regression. They are composed of three layers: an input layer, a hidden layer with radial basis functions (often Gaussian functions), and an output layer. RBF networks are typically used when the relationship between inputs and outputs is highly non-linear.

- **Applications**: RBF networks are useful in **classification**, **regression**, and **time-series prediction**, particularly when the data has a high degree of non-linearity.

Long Short-Term Memory (LSTM) Networks

Long Short-Term Memory (LSTM) networks are an advanced type of RNN designed to overcome the vanishing gradient problem.

LSTMs use memory cells to maintain long-term dependencies in sequences, making them highly effective for tasks like speech recognition and natural language processing.

- **How LSTMs Work**: LSTMs use specialized gating mechanisms (input, forget, and output gates) to control the flow of information into and out of the memory cells. This allows them to retain information over long periods, effectively learning long-range dependencies.

  Applications: LSTMs excel in sequential data tasks such as **machine translation**, **speech recognition**, and **time-series forecasting**, where the context of earlier data points is essential for prediction.

Training Neural Networks

- **Loss Functions**
    - o Mean squared error, cross-entropy, and other loss functions.
- **Optimization Algorithms**
    - o Stochastic Gradient Descent (SGD), Adam, Adagrad, and others.
- **Overfitting and Regularization**
    - o Techniques like dropout, L2 regularization, and cross-validation.
- **Hyperparameter Tuning**
    - o Learning rates, batch sizes, number of layers, etc.

Training Neural Networks

Training neural networks is the cornerstone of building effective machine learning models. This chapter expands on the core aspects of the training process, including how to define the **loss function**, select the right **optimization algorithms**, prevent **overfitting**, and perform **hyperparameter tuning**. These are the foundational components that influence the accuracy, generalization, and efficiency of a neural network. Mastering these concepts will allow you to train neural networks effectively, whether you're working on image classification, natural language processing, or any other machine learning task.

1. Loss Functions

The **loss function** serves as a critical indicator of how well the neural network is performing. During training, the goal is to minimize this loss, which reflects the difference between the predicted output of the network and the actual target values. Choosing the right loss function is essential because it directly influences the optimization process and the overall performance of the model.

Common Loss Functions in Detail

- **Mean Squared Error (MSE):**
    - **Why It Works**: MSE is simple and intuitive. It's commonly used in **regression tasks**, where you are predicting continuous values (such as predicting a house's price based on features like square footage or neighborhood).
    - **Real-world Example**: Consider a model predicting the temperature of a city based on historical data. The MSE

loss will quantify the difference between the predicted temperatures and the actual measured temperatures.

Formula:

$$MSE = \frac{1}{N} \sum_{i=1}^{N} (y^i_{pred} - y^i_{true})^2$$

where N is the number of data points, and y_{pred}, y_{true} are the predicted and actual values, respectively.

Pros: Easy to compute and effective for many regression tasks. It punishes large errors more severely due to the squaring operation, which can help the model focus on reducing larger mistakes.

Cons: Sensitive to outliers in the data, which may skew the model's learning process.

- **Cross-Entropy Loss**:
  - o **Why It Works**: Cross-entropy loss is commonly used for **classification tasks**, particularly when the output of the neural network is categorical (e.g., classifying an image as either a cat or a dog).

Formula:

$$H(p, q) = - \sum_{i=1}^{C} y^i_{true} \log(y^i_{pred})$$

where C is the number of classes, $y_{i true}$ is the true class label (usually in one-hot encoded format), and y_{pred} is the predicted probability for each class.

Real-world Example: Imagine a model trained to classify whether an email is spam or not. Using cross-entropy, the network penalizes its predictions based on how far off the predicted class probabilities are from the actual binary outcome (spam or not spam).

Pros: Ideal for classification problems, particularly in multi-class or multi-label classification. It provides probabilities for each class, making it well-suited for scenarios where you need to output class probabilities (e.g., medical diagnosis where multiple classes are possible).

Cons: Can be computationally expensive, particularly for large datasets with many classes.

- **Other Loss Functions**:
  - **Hinge Loss**: Used for binary classification tasks, particularly with **Support Vector Machines (SVMs)**. It penalizes misclassifications and encourages the model to maximize the margin between the decision boundary and the data points.
  - **Huber Loss**: A combination of MSE and absolute error, Huber loss is more robust to outliers than MSE. It uses MSE for smaller errors and absolute error for larger errors, making it particularly useful for noisy regression tasks.

Choosing the Right Loss Function

The loss function should align with the type of problem you're solving:

- For **regression** problems, where the output is continuous, **Mean Squared Error** is often the best choice.
- For **classification** problems, particularly with binary or multi-class labels, **Cross-Entropy Loss** is typically preferred.
- **Huber loss** and **hinge loss** are excellent for cases where you want to be more robust to outliers or when working with support

vector machines.

2. Optimization Algorithms

Once the loss function is defined, the next crucial step is to minimize it by optimizing the network's weights. This is achieved through **optimization algorithms** that adjust the model's parameters iteratively to reduce the loss.

Stochastic Gradient Descent (SGD)

- **Description**: **Stochastic Gradient Descent (SGD)** is the backbone of most neural network training. It updates the network's parameters by calculating the gradient of the loss function with respect to each parameter, and then taking small steps in the opposite direction (gradient descent) to minimize the loss. The term "stochastic" refers to the fact that it uses a random subset of data (a mini-batch) to compute each gradient, rather than the entire dataset.
- **How It Works**:
  - Compute the gradient of the loss with respect to the weights.
  - Update weights by subtracting a fraction of the gradient (scaled by the **learning rate**).
- **Advantages**: SGD can be faster than batch gradient descent because it processes a small subset of data at each iteration, making it suitable for large datasets.
- **Challenges**: The randomness in updates can cause the path to the optimal solution to be noisy, potentially leading to longer convergence times or suboptimal solutions.

Adam (Adaptive Moment Estimation)

- **Description**: **Adam** combines the best of two worlds: the benefits of both **AdaGrad** (which adapts the learning rate for each parameter) and **RMSProp** (which smoothes the gradients). It calculates first-order (mean) and second-order (uncentered variance) moments of the gradients and adjusts the learning rate accordingly.
- **How It Works**:
  - Adam keeps track of moving averages of both the **first moment** (mean) and **second moment** (variance) of the gradients.
  - The optimizer uses these averages to adapt the learning rates for each weight during the training process.
- **Advantages**: Adam often performs better and converges faster than SGD, especially for complex models like deep networks. It is robust to the choice of hyperparameters and can handle noisy gradients.
- **Challenges**: Although Adam is generally effective, it requires tuning the hyperparameters such as the learning rate, which can still be computationally expensive.

Adagrad and Adadelta

- **Adagrad**: **Adagrad** dynamically adjusts the learning rate for each parameter based on the frequency of updates. Parameters with more frequent updates will receive smaller learning rates, and those with infrequent updates will receive larger learning rates.
- **Adadelta**: **Adadelta** is an improvement on Adagrad. Instead of accumulating all historical gradients, it keeps a moving

average of the squared gradients to prevent the learning rate from decaying too quickly.

- **Advantages**: These optimizers are particularly useful for sparse data, such as text data in natural language processing, where some features appear far less frequently than others.
- **Challenges**: These optimizers can lead to overly conservative updates, especially when working with large datasets or when the model requires a more aggressive learning rate.

Choosing the Right Optimizer

- For **large datasets** or **complex models**, **Adam** is often the best choice because it converges quickly and adapts the learning rate dynamically.
- For **simpler models** or when computational efficiency is important, **SGD** may still be a valid choice.
- **Adagrad** and **Adadelta** are ideal when working with **sparse data**.

3. Overfitting and Regularization

Overfitting is a common problem in training neural networks where the model learns to memorize the training data, including its noise and errors, rather than learning the general patterns. Overfitting typically occurs when the model is too complex for the amount of data available. Regularization techniques are used to prevent overfitting by simplifying the model and improving its ability to generalize to new data.

Regularization Techniques

- **Dropout**:
  - **Description**: Dropout involves randomly setting a fraction of the neurons to zero during training. This prevents the network from becoming too reliant on specific neurons and encourages it to learn more robust, generalized features.
  - **How It Works**: At each training step, a random subset of neurons is "dropped out," and their outputs are set to zero. This forces the network to find alternate ways to represent the information.

  Pros: Dropout has proven particularly effective in deep neural networks, including CNNs and RNNs. It is a simple and highly effective way to prevent overfitting.

  Cons: It can slow down training since more epochs may be needed to converge.

- **L2 Regularization (Ridge Regularization)**:
  - **Description**: L2 regularization adds a penalty term to the loss function based on the squared weights. This encourages smaller weights, preventing any one feature from dominating the learning process.

  Formula:

  $$L2 = \lambda \sum_i w_i^2$$

  where λ is the regularization parameter, and w_i are the model weights.

73

Pros: L2 regularization tends to work well in models where the number of features is large, and it encourages the model to learn weights that are small and not too biased.

Cons: The regularization term can make the model less expressive if it is too strong, potentially leading to underfitting.

- **Cross-Validation**:
  - **Description**: Cross-validation involves splitting the data into multiple subsets (or "folds") and training the model multiple times, each time using different subsets for training and testing. This allows you to evaluate how well the model generalizes to unseen data.

Real-world Example: In machine learning competitions, cross-validation is often used to validate models and ensure that they are not overfitting to the training set.

Pros: Helps in detecting overfitting and provides a more reliable estimate of model performance.

Cons: It can be computationally expensive because it requires training multiple models.

Choosing Regularization Techniques

- Use **dropout** in deep networks (like CNNs) where overfitting is likely due to the large number of parameters.
- **L2 regularization** is useful for preventing overfitting in networks with many parameters, especially when the data contains noise.
- **Cross-validation** is a key technique to assess model generalization and to select the best model configuration.

4. Hyperparameter Tuning

The process of **hyperparameter tuning** involves finding the best set of parameters that control the training process, including the learning rate, batch size, and the architecture of the network. These parameters are not learned from the data directly but are set before training begins. Effective tuning is often the key to achieving optimal performance.

Common Hyperparameters to Tune

- **Learning Rate**: Controls the step size during gradient descent. Too large a learning rate can lead to oscillations, while too small a learning rate can make convergence slow.
- **Batch Size**: Refers to the number of data samples used in each iteration of training. A smaller batch size provides more frequent updates, but a larger batch size tends to make training more stable.
- **Number of Layers**: The depth of the neural network is crucial for its performance. More layers typically mean the model can learn more complex patterns but can also lead to overfitting if not regularized properly.
- **Momentum**: Momentum helps the optimizer accelerate in the relevant direction and dampen oscillations. It is particularly useful for speeding up convergence in SGD.

Hyperparameter Tuning Methods

- **Grid Search**: Try all combinations of hyperparameters from a predefined set and evaluate the model for each. This is exhaustive but computationally expensive.
- **Random Search**: Instead of testing every possible combination, randomly sample hyperparameters from predefined ranges. It's computationally less expensive and can find optimal solutions faster.
- **Bayesian Optimization**: A more sophisticated method that models the objective function and intelligently explores the hyperparameter space.

Deep Learning

- **What is Deep Learning?**
  - o Difference between shallow and deep neural networks.
- **Deep Architectures**
  - o Deep feedforward networks, deep convolutional networks, and deep recurrent networks.
- **Transfer Learning**
  - o Using pre-trained models for new tasks.

Deep Learning

Deep learning represents one of the most exciting and transformative developments in artificial intelligence (AI) and machine learning. With its ability to learn from large amounts of data, deep learning has enabled breakthroughs in diverse fields, from self-driving cars and robotics to healthcare and entertainment. This chapter provides a detailed exploration of deep learning, covering fundamental concepts, deep architectures, and the growing field of transfer learning.

1. What is Deep Learning?

Deep learning is a subset of machine learning that utilizes artificial neural networks with many layers (hence the term "deep") to analyze various forms of data. The core advantage of deep learning is its capacity to automatically learn representations from data, reducing the need for manual feature extraction. This makes it particularly well-suited for tasks involving complex, high-dimensional data such as images, text, audio, and video.

Shallow vs. Deep Neural Networks

To understand deep learning fully, it's important to differentiate between **shallow** and **deep neural networks**. The distinction primarily lies in the depth (number of layers) of the neural network, which impacts its ability to model and understand data.

- **Shallow Neural Networks**:
    - **Characteristics**: A shallow neural network typically consists of a single hidden layer between the input and output. These networks can model simple, linearly separable problems, making them suitable for tasks like basic classification or regression on relatively simple datasets.
    - **Limitations**: Shallow networks struggle to capture more complex structures in data. They can't efficiently process hierarchical relationships in data, like the spatial structure in images or temporal relationships in text and speech.
- **Deep Neural Networks**:
    - **Characteristics**: Deep neural networks, by contrast, consist of multiple hidden layers, which allow them to create hierarchical representations of the data. In these networks, the first few layers detect simple features, such as edges or corners, and as the layers go deeper, the network begins to recognize more abstract patterns, such as shapes, objects, or concepts.
    - **How Deep Learning Works**: For example, in a deep learning network tasked with classifying images, the first layers might detect edges, the middle layers might detect shapes (like circles or rectangles), and the deepest layers might recognize high-level concepts like a "cat" or "dog." This layered feature extraction enables deep learning models to handle far more complex tasks compared to shallow networks.

Real-World Analogy: Imagine teaching a child to recognize a chair. Initially, they might be taught to look for general shapes like rectangles. As they grow and experience more examples, they begin to understand the details—like the four legs, seat, and backrest—that make up a chair. This analogy reflects how deep neural networks learn features at different levels.

2. Deep Architectures

Deep learning uses several specialized architectures to process specific types of data effectively. Let's explore the three primary deep learning architectures: **deep feedforward networks (DNNs)**, **convolutional neural networks (CNNs)**, and **recurrent neural networks (RNNs)**.

Deep Feedforward Networks (DNNs)

Deep feedforward networks are the most basic type of deep neural network. Information in a DNN flows in one direction—from the input layer through hidden layers to the output layer—without any feedback loops. These networks are sometimes called **fully connected networks** because each neuron in one layer is connected to every neuron in the next layer.

- **How It Works**: During training, DNNs learn to adjust the weights of connections between neurons to minimize the **loss function**, which measures the difference between the predicted output and the true output.
- **Applications**: DNNs are commonly used in tasks where input-output relationships are relatively simple and don't require specialized processing. These tasks include:
  - **Regression**: Predicting continuous values, such as predicting a person's weight based on height and age.
  - **Classification**: Determining whether an image is of a cat or a dog (although CNNs are more commonly used for image tasks).
- **Strengths**: DNNs are versatile and can be used for a wide range of problems. However, as datasets grow in complexity, their limitations in capturing intricate patterns become apparent, and more specialized architectures like CNNs and RNNs are often preferred.

Deep Convolutional Networks (CNNs)

Convolutional Neural Networks (CNNs) are specialized deep learning architectures designed to work with **grid-like data,** such as images or video. Unlike DNNs, which treat all input features equally, CNNs use local connectivity and shared weights, which allow them to detect spatial hierarchies in data.

- **How CNNs Work**: CNNs are made up of several types of layers:
    - **Convolutional layers**: These layers apply convolutional filters (also called kernels) to the input data. The filters slide over the input image and detect low-level features such as edges, textures, and shapes.
    - **Pooling layers**: After the convolution, pooling layers down-sample the data by selecting the most important features, which reduces the dimensionality and helps the network focus on the most relevant parts of the image.
    - **Fully connected layers**: At the end of the network, fully connected layers are used to make final predictions based on the features learned from earlier layers.
- **Applications**:
    - **Image recognition**: Identifying objects in an image (e.g., classifying images of animals, detecting faces).
    - **Object detection**: Locating objects within an image and classifying them (e.g., detecting pedestrians in autonomous vehicle systems).
    - **Medical image analysis**: Detecting tumors in MRI or CT scan images.
- **Why CNNs Are Effective**: CNNs excel at capturing spatial hierarchies in images. Instead of requiring manually crafted features (like edges, corners, or textures), CNNs automatically learn to recognize these features through training. This capability makes CNNs highly effective for a wide range of computer vision tasks.

Real-World Example: A self-driving car uses CNNs to process data from its cameras to identify objects like pedestrians, traffic signs, and other vehicles. By detecting these objects, the car can make decisions, like when to stop or swerve.

Deep Recurrent Networks (RNNs)

Recurrent Neural Networks (RNNs) are designed for sequential data, where the order of information matters. Unlike feedforward networks, RNNs have **feedback loops** that allow information to persist over time, enabling the network to "remember" previous inputs and maintain context.

- **How RNNs Work**: RNNs process one input at a time, updating the hidden state with each new input. This allows the network to retain knowledge of prior inputs, making it well-suited for tasks where the context or order of inputs is critical.
- **Applications**:
    - **Natural language processing**: For example, generating text, machine translation, or sentiment analysis. RNNs process one word at a time in a sentence and use context from previous words to make predictions.
    - **Speech recognition**: Converting spoken language into text by considering the temporal patterns in sound waves.
    - **Time-series forecasting**: Predicting future values based on historical data (e.g., stock market prices, weather forecasting).

- **Challenges with RNNs**: One of the major challenges in training traditional RNNs is the **vanishing gradient problem,** where the gradients used to update weights become too small during backpropagation, causing the network to forget earlier inputs. This issue can be addressed by using advanced types of RNNs, such as **Long Short-Term Memory (LSTM)** networks or **Gated Recurrent Units (GRU)**.

Real-World Example: RNNs power the speech recognition system in virtual assistants like Siri or Alexa. These systems listen to user commands, convert spoken words into text, and then use that text to process and respond intelligently.

3. Transfer Learning

One of the major advancements in deep learning in recent years is **transfer learning**—the ability to leverage pre-trained models on one task and adapt them for use on another, related task. Transfer learning significantly reduces the amount of data and computational power required to train deep learning models, allowing even smaller organizations or teams to build powerful AI systems.

How Transfer Learning Works

Transfer learning works by taking a model that has already been trained on a large, diverse dataset (usually a dataset that is similar to the problem you are solving) and adapting it to your specific task. This process often involves **fine-tuning** the model to adjust it to the new task, usually by modifying the last few layers of the network and re-training them with a smaller dataset.

- **Steps in Transfer Learning**:
    1. **Pre-training**: Start with a model that has been pre-trained on a large, generalized dataset (for example, a model trained on the ImageNet dataset, which contains millions of images).
    2. **Fine-tuning**: Replace the output layers with new layers suited for your task, and train the model using your specific dataset. This process involves adjusting the weights of the model slightly to make it perform well on the new task.
    3. **Freezing Layers**: In many cases, the earlier layers of the pre-trained model are already good at extracting low-level features like edges or textures, so these layers are frozen (i.e., not trained). Only the higher layers are fine-tuned on the new dataset.
- **Applications of Transfer Learning**:

    - **Image Classification**: A model pre-trained on ImageNet can be fine-tuned to classify images from a specialized dataset, such as medical images or product images for e-commerce.
    - **Natural Language Processing (NLP)**: Models like **BERT** and **GPT** have been pre-trained on massive text corpora and can be fine-tuned to tasks like sentiment analysis or question answering.
    - **Speech-to-Text**: A pre-trained model trained on a large speech dataset can be fine-tuned to recognize accents or speech patterns specific to a particular region or industry.

Benefits of Transfer Learning

- **Faster Training**: Since you're leveraging an already pre-trained model, you don't have to train from scratch, which dramatically reduces both the time and computational resources required.

- **Improved Performance**: By building on a model trained on a large dataset, transfer learning allows the model to benefit from features that have already been learned, often leading to better performance on the new task, especially when the new dataset is small.
- **Less Data**: Transfer learning can be especially useful in domains where labeled data is scarce. Instead of needing a huge dataset to train a deep model, you can use the large amount of data available for pre-training to overcome the lack of data in your own domain.

Applications of Neural Networks

- **Computer Vision**
  - o Image classification, object detection, segmentation.
- **Natural Language Processing (NLP)**
  - o Text classification, sentiment analysis, machine translation.
- **Speech Recognition**
  - o Converting speech to text and understanding audio signals.
- **Reinforcement Learning**
  - o Neural networks in decision-making, robotics, and gaming.

Applications of Neural Networks

Neural networks have transformed the way we solve complex problems across various domains by learning patterns from data and making intelligent decisions. From healthcare to entertainment, autonomous systems, and natural language processing (NLP), neural networks have enabled innovations that were once thought to be impossible. This chapter delves deeper into the diverse and groundbreaking applications of neural networks, exploring how they are revolutionizing fields like **computer vision**, **natural language processing (NLP)**, **speech recognition**, and **reinforcement learning**.

1. Computer Vision

Computer vision is the field of AI that focuses on enabling machines to interpret and understand the visual world. Neural networks, especially **Convolutional Neural Networks (CNNs)**, have made remarkable progress in enabling computers to analyze and interpret images and videos.

Image Classification

Image classification is the task of categorizing an image into one of several predefined classes based on its content. The accuracy and efficiency of image classification systems are critical in many real-world applications.

- **How Neural Networks Solve Image Classification**: Convolutional Neural Networks (CNNs) have become the go-to architecture for image classification. The network is made up of layers that gradually extract features from the raw pixel values of an image. Early layers might detect basic features such as edges, textures, or color, while deeper layers combine these features into more abstract representations such as shapes and objects.

- **Real-World Example**: **ImageNet**, one of the largest image datasets, contains millions of labeled images from thousands of categories. CNNs trained on this dataset can classify images with high accuracy. Such models have been adopted in a wide range of applications, from identifying objects in digital photos to detecting medical conditions in radiological images (e.g., classifying a brain scan as showing signs of a tumor).

Object Detection

Object detection goes beyond classification by not only identifying objects in an image but also locating them by drawing bounding boxes around each object. This task is crucial for any application where identifying and localizing objects is important.

- **How It Works**: Advanced neural networks like **YOLO (You Only Look Once)** and **Faster R-CNN** are designed to predict both the class of objects (like a cat or car) and the position of those objects within an image. These models are trained to identify and classify multiple objects in a single image while keeping track of their location.
- **Real-World Example**: **Autonomous vehicles** use object detection to navigate safely by identifying pedestrians, other vehicles, road signs, and obstacles. This technology helps cars make real-time decisions, such as when to stop or when to swerve, thereby ensuring safe driving.

Image Segmentation

Image segmentation divides an image into meaningful parts, often corresponding to distinct objects or object parts. This is especially useful in tasks that require understanding the exact boundaries of objects in an image.

- **How Neural Networks Enable Segmentation**: **Fully Convolutional Networks (FCNs)** and **U–Net** are common neural network architectures for semantic segmentation. These networks classify each pixel in an image, assigning it a label corresponding to the object it belongs to, resulting in a detailed pixel-wise segmentation map.
- **Real-World Example**: In **medical imaging**, segmentation is crucial for accurately identifying and delineating structures like tumors or organs in MRI or CT scans. This allows for better diagnosis and treatment planning, particularly in cancer detection and surgery planning.

2. Natural Language Processing (NLP)

Natural Language Processing (NLP) is the branch of AI that focuses on the interaction between computers and human languages. The advancements in neural networks have made NLP tasks, such as text analysis and machine translation, much more efficient and accurate.

Text Classification

Text classification is the task of categorizing text into predefined categories, such as spam detection, topic categorization, or sentiment analysis. Neural networks are widely used to automatically learn the features that help classify text into the right categories.

- **How Neural Networks Handle Text Classification**: Modern NLP models use **word embeddings** (dense vector representations of words) to capture semantic meaning. **LSTMs (Long Short-Term Memory networks)** and **transformers** like **BERT (Bidirectional Encoder Representations from Transformers)** process the sequences of words and learn context from surrounding words to make accurate predictions.

- **Real-World Example**: **Email spam filters** use text classification models to detect and block unwanted emails based on their content. Similarly, **content recommendation systems** (like those used by news outlets and social media platforms) categorize articles and recommend them to users based on their interests.

Sentiment Analysis

Sentiment analysis involves determining the emotional tone behind a piece of text—whether the text expresses positive, negative, or neutral sentiments. It's widely used by businesses to analyze customer feedback, reviews, and social media comments.

- **How It Works**: NLP models like **BERT** and **GPT** use deep learning to understand not only the words in a sentence but also their context. These models learn to identify subtle linguistic cues such as sarcasm, tone, and emotions, making sentiment analysis more accurate than ever before.
- **Real-World Example**: **Brand reputation management** companies use sentiment analysis to scan social media platforms and product reviews to measure how customers feel about a brand. This helps companies adapt their marketing strategies, improve customer service, and address any negative feedback.

Machine Translation

Machine translation is the process of translating text from one language to another. Neural networks have revolutionized this task by significantly improving translation quality, especially in complex, context-dependent languages.

- **How Neural Networks Improve Machine Translation**: **Sequence-to-sequence models**, which include **LSTMs** and **transformers**, are designed to convert one sequence (like a sentence in English) into another sequence (a translation in French or Chinese). The **attention mechanism** in transformer models enables better translation by focusing on relevant parts of the sentence at each step, allowing for more fluent and accurate translations.
- **Real-World Example**: **Google Translate** and other translation services like **DeepL** now offer near-instant translations for dozens of languages, making it easier for people to communicate across language barriers. In industries such as e-commerce and customer support, machine translation helps bridge linguistic gaps, expanding market reach and improving global communication.

3. Speech Recognition

Speech recognition refers to the technology that enables machines to convert spoken language into text. Neural networks, particularly **RNNs (Recurrent Neural Networks)** and **LSTMs**, have significantly improved speech recognition systems by learning how to understand various accents, speech patterns, and noise.

Converting Speech to Text

Converting speech into text involves recognizing individual phonemes (the smallest units of sound) and understanding how these phonemes combine to form words and sentences.

- **How Neural Networks Enable Speech Recognition**: Deep learning models take raw audio input and convert it into a sequence of features that represent speech. These features are then processed by neural networks, which map them to the corresponding text. Advanced systems use LSTMs and **CNNs** to handle temporal relationships in speech data and improve recognition accuracy, especially in noisy environments.
- **Real-World Example**: **Virtual assistants** like **Siri, Alexa,** and **Google Assistant** rely on neural networks to convert voice commands into actionable tasks. These systems are trained to understand various accents and respond to a wide range of requests, from setting reminders to controlling smart home devices.

Understanding Audio Signals

Beyond speech-to-text conversion, neural networks are also used to understand complex audio signals, such as identifying speakers or detecting emotions from speech.

- **How Neural Networks Help Understand Audio**: Neural networks can be trained to recognize speaker identities (speaker recognition) or detect emotional tones in speech (emotion recognition). **Deep learning models** process audio signals to extract features such as pitch, tone, and cadence, and learn patterns that distinguish different speakers or emotional states.
- **Real-World Example**: In **call center automation**, speech recognition systems can transcribe customer calls and analyze the emotional tone of customers' voices. This helps businesses understand customer sentiments and provide more personalized support. In healthcare, speech emotion recognition can be used to monitor patients' mental health based on their speech patterns.

4. Reinforcement Learning

Reinforcement Learning (RL) is a type of machine learning where an agent learns to make decisions by interacting with an environment. Neural networks have been instrumental in enabling RL to solve complex, high-dimensional decision-making problems.

Neural Networks in Decision-Making

In reinforcement learning, agents learn through trial and error, receiving feedback in the form of rewards or penalties. Neural networks are used to approximate the decision-making function (the policy or the Q-value function) that maximizes rewards for an agent over time.

- **How Neural Networks Enable RL**: **Deep Q-Networks (DQN)** use neural networks to approximate the Q-value function, which predicts the expected future reward for each action taken in a given state. This allows the agent to learn an optimal policy (the best set of actions) for maximizing rewards over time.
- **Real-World Example**: **Robotic arms** used in manufacturing can be trained with RL to perform precise assembly tasks. By interacting with the environment, the robot learns the best strategies for picking up, positioning, and assembling parts.

Reinforcement Learning in Gaming

Reinforcement learning has also been used in gaming to train agents to make decisions that optimize performance. RL agents can play games repeatedly, using the rewards from successful actions to improve their strategies.

- **How RL Works in Games**: One of the most famous examples of RL is **AlphaGo**, an AI developed by Google DeepMind that used deep reinforcement learning to learn how to play the ancient game of Go. Through self-play, AlphaGo became stronger than the world's top human Go players.
- **Real-World Example**: **OpenAI's Dota 2 AI** (OpenAI Five) is another breakthrough example of RL. This AI used reinforcement learning to master the complex multiplayer game Dota 2. By playing against itself, it learned to make strategic decisions, outperforming human players in the game.

Challenges and Ethical Considerations

- **Bias and Fairness in AI**
  - How biases emerge in training data and how to mitigate them.
- **Explainability and Interpretability**
  - Why neural networks are often seen as "black-box" models.
- **Energy Consumption**
  - The environmental impact of training large models.

Challenges and Ethical Considerations in Neural Networks

As neural networks continue to evolve and influence a wide array of industries, the ethical challenges that accompany their development and deployment have become increasingly apparent. While the power and potential of artificial intelligence (AI) and deep learning technologies are undeniable, their application brings forth a number of serious considerations that demand attention. From ensuring fairness to addressing transparency, and from minimizing their environmental impact to confronting issues of accountability, the conversation around ethical AI is growing louder. This extended discussion focuses on the key challenges and ethical concerns associated with neural networks, delving deeper into **bias and fairness**, **explainability and interpretability**, and **energy consumption**. By exploring these topics in detail, we can better understand the complex ethical landscape of neural networks and work toward more responsible AI development.

1. Bias and Fairness in AI

The problem of **bias in AI** is one of the most pressing concerns in the field of neural networks. As neural networks are trained on vast amounts of historical data, they can inadvertently learn and perpetuate the biases that exist in those data sets. These biases, if left unchecked, can lead to unfair outcomes that negatively impact underrepresented or marginalized groups. The consequences of such biases in AI applications can be wide-reaching, affecting everything from hiring practices to criminal justice systems. Therefore, addressing bias and ensuring fairness is crucial to the responsible deployment of neural networks.

How Bias Emerges in Training Data

- **Historical Bias**: This occurs when historical data reflects discriminatory or prejudiced behavior. For instance, a facial recognition system trained predominantly on images of white people will be less accurate when attempting to recognize faces of people from other racial backgrounds. Historical bias can also emerge in predictive systems used in criminal justice, healthcare, and hiring practices, where data may reflect societal inequalities.
- **Sampling Bias**: Neural networks are only as good as the data they are trained on. If a model is trained on unrepresentative or incomplete data, it may not generalize well to the broader population. Sampling bias arises when certain groups or conditions are overrepresented or underrepresented in training datasets. This leads to skewed models that may perform better for some groups while disadvantaging others.
- **Measurement Bias**: In some cases, bias is introduced not through the data itself, but through how the data is collected or measured. For example, a predictive model that analyzes the likelihood of criminal recidivism may be biased if the underlying crime statistics are influenced by biased law enforcement practices or selective policing.

Mitigating Bias in AI

To address the problem of bias in neural networks, several approaches can be applied, both at the level of data collection and model training:

- **Bias Detection and Auditing**: A critical step in mitigating bias is identifying it early in the process. Data auditing tools such as IBM's **AI Fairness 360** or Google's **What-If Tool** allow developers to test models for fairness and bias. These tools can assess how different groups are affected by the model and identify any disparities in the predictions or outcomes based on protected attributes (e.g., race, gender, etc.).
- **Fair Data Collection**: Ensuring that data collection processes are fair and representative of all groups is essential. This includes making concerted efforts to gather data from underrepresented communities and using data augmentation techniques to balance datasets. In areas like healthcare, where biased data could lead to unequal treatment, it is crucial to ensure that the data represents diverse populations.
- **Fairness-Aware Algorithms**: Incorporating fairness constraints into the learning process can help ensure that neural networks make decisions that are equitable for all. Approaches like **adversarial debiasing** and **counterfactual fairness** are designed to reduce bias in machine learning models. These algorithms try to minimize the disparity between outcomes for different groups without sacrificing the overall performance of the model.

- **Human-in-the-Loop (HITL)**: In high-stakes applications, such as hiring, criminal justice, or lending, it is essential to incorporate human judgment into the decision-making process. Human-in-the-loop approaches allow humans to review and intervene in decisions made by AI systems, ensuring that biases are detected and corrected before they lead to unfair outcomes.
- **Ethical Guidelines and Policies**: Policymakers and organizations are beginning to establish ethical frameworks and guidelines to address AI fairness. These guidelines advocate for the development of models that are both accurate and fair and encourage transparency in how AI systems are trained, evaluated, and deployed.

2. Explainability and Interpretability

Neural networks, particularly deep learning models, are often considered **black-box** models due to their complexity and the opacity of their decision-making processes. While these models can achieve high accuracy and outperform traditional machine learning models in many tasks, their lack of explainability raises concerns, especially in critical applications where understanding the reasoning behind AI decisions is necessary for accountability and trust.

Why Neural Networks Are Seen as "Black-Box" Models

- **Layered Complexity**: The architecture of deep neural networks involves many layers of interconnected neurons, each performing non-linear transformations on the data. These transformations result in abstract representations of the input, making it challenging to reverse-engineer or interpret how each input feature contributes to the final prediction.
- **Non-Linear Activations**: The introduction of non-linear activation functions, such as **ReLU** or **sigmoid**, helps neural networks learn complex patterns in data. However, these non-linear transformations make the decision-making process less transparent, as small changes in the input can lead to unpredictable changes in the output, complicating efforts to understand how a model arrived at its decision.
- **High-Dimensional Data**: Neural networks are often trained on high-dimensional data (e.g., images, speech, or text), which involves processing thousands or even millions of features. The relationships between these features are often too intricate and complex to be easily interpreted by humans.

Improving Explainability and Interpretability

Efforts to improve the explainability of neural networks focus on making the internal workings of these models more transparent, allowing users and stakeholders to understand how decisions are made.

- **Local Explainability Techniques**: **LIME (Local Interpretable Model-agnostic Explanations)** and **SHAP (SHapley Additive exPlanations)** are techniques that help explain individual predictions made by a neural network. These approaches generate interpretable approximations of the model's decision process by focusing on specific instances and showing how individual features influenced the prediction.
- **Visualization Techniques**: In models like **Convolutional Neural Networks (CNNs)**, researchers use visualization techniques to understand the features learned by different layers. **Feature maps** and **saliency maps** provide insight into which parts of an image were most important for classification. Similarly, in NLP models, attention mechanisms highlight which words in a sentence are most significant for the model's output, offering a glimpse into the decision-making process.
- **Post-Hoc Interpretability**: Post-hoc interpretability techniques analyze trained models after they've made predictions. For example, **Layer-wise Relevance Propagation (LRP)** helps identify which neurons and layers in a neural network contributed most to a given prediction. Such tools can shed light on the inner workings of a neural network, making it easier to spot potential issues like overfitting or bias.

- **Transparent Models**: Some researchers are working to design inherently interpretable models. For example, **Decision Trees**, **Rule-Based Systems**, and simpler models like **Logistic Regression** are often preferred in situations where interpretability is paramount, as they provide more transparent decision-making processes than complex neural networks.
- **Regulatory Requirements**: In industries like finance and healthcare, regulatory bodies may demand that AI systems be interpretable, particularly when they are used in high-stakes decision-making. Legal frameworks like the **EU's General Data Protection Regulation (GDPR)** and **the right to explanation** require that individuals can understand the reasoning behind decisions that significantly affect them, such as loan rejections or medical diagnoses.

3. Energy Consumption and Environmental Impact

The training of deep learning models, especially large-scale models with billions of parameters, requires significant computational power. This, in turn, leads to substantial **energy consumption**. As neural networks grow more complex, so does their demand for energy, raising concerns about their environmental impact and sustainability. The increasing carbon footprint of AI development and deployment has prompted calls for more energy-efficient practices and sustainable AI practices.

The Environmental Impact of Training Large Models

- **High Computational Demand**: Modern neural networks, such as **transformer-based models** (e.g., GPT-3, BERT) and **vision transformers**, require immense computational resources to train. These models are trained on high-performance GPUs or TPUs, which can run 24/7 for weeks at a time, consuming vast amounts of electricity. For example, training a large transformer model can consume the same amount of energy as an entire country for several months.
- **Carbon Footprint of Data Centers**: The environmental impact of training large models extends beyond just the computational resources; it also includes the energy used to power and cool data centers. While some companies, such as Google and Microsoft, have made efforts to transition to renewable energy, many data centers still rely on fossil fuels, contributing to the carbon emissions associated with AI training.
- **Energy-Intensive Training Cycles**: Models like GPT-3, which contains over 175 billion parameters, are trained on massive datasets and require many iterations (epochs) to converge. Each iteration involves millions of calculations, consuming a significant amount of energy. In fact, some studies estimate that training GPT-3 could emit as much CO_2 as five cars over their entire lifetimes.

Mitigating Energy Consumption in AI

To reduce the environmental impact of neural network training, several solutions are being explored:

- **Efficient Training Techniques**: Researchers are investigating ways to make training algorithms more efficient, reducing the number of computations required. Techniques like **model distillation**, where a smaller model learns from a larger one, or **quantization**, which reduces the precision of computations, can significantly reduce the computational load.
- **Energy-Efficient Hardware**: The development of specialized AI hardware, such as **custom-designed AI chips** (e.g., TPUs), offers the potential for more energy-efficient training. These chips are optimized for deep learning tasks, making them more power-efficient than general-purpose processors like CPUs or GPUs.
- **Sustainable Data Centers**: Companies are increasingly moving toward **green data centers**, which are powered by renewable energy sources like wind or solar. Additionally, optimizing the cooling systems and reducing unnecessary energy consumption in data centers can also play a key role in minimizing the environmental footprint.
- **Smarter AI Models**: Researchers are also focusing on developing smaller, more efficient neural network models that require fewer computational resources to train and deploy. Techniques like **sparse models** (which use fewer parameters) and **early stopping** (which halts training once a model reaches acceptable performance) can help reduce energy usage without sacrificing accuracy.

- **Carbon Offsetting and Accountability**: Some AI companies are beginning to offset the carbon emissions generated by their operations by investing in renewable energy projects or carbon capture initiatives. These efforts can help neutralize the environmental impact of AI development, making the industry more sustainable.

Practical Implementation

- **Setting Up a Neural Network**
  - o Popular libraries: TensorFlow, PyTorch, Keras.
- **Training Models**
  - o Hands-on examples and code snippets.
- **Optimization and Debugging**
  - o Debugging model training, tuning for better performance.
- **Deploying Models**
  - o Moving from training to deployment in real-world applications.

Practical Implementation of Neural Networks

This chapter focuses on the practical implementation of neural networks, guiding you through the entire process—from setting up a neural network, training it effectively, optimizing for better performance, debugging, and finally deploying the model into real-world applications. Building and deploying neural networks can be complex, but with the right tools and techniques, it becomes manageable and efficient. We'll walk you through the best practices and provide detailed examples, code snippets, and explanations for each stage of the implementation pipeline. This chapter will ensure you not only understand how to build and train neural networks but also how to bring them into production.

1. Setting Up a Neural Network

Before we dive into training, it's essential to have a clear understanding of the libraries and frameworks commonly used to build and deploy neural networks. These libraries abstract away much of the complexity involved in designing and training a neural network, allowing you to focus on the architecture and model performance.

Popular Libraries: TensorFlow, PyTorch, Keras

- **TensorFlow**: TensorFlow is one of the most widely-used open-source machine learning frameworks, developed by Google Brain. It provides a comprehensive ecosystem for building and deploying neural networks at scale. TensorFlow's flexibility allows it to be used across various platforms and devices, from mobile to high-performance cloud environments. With TensorFlow 2.0, the integration of Keras as the high-level API simplifies model development while retaining TensorFlow's powerful capabilities.

  Advantages of TensorFlow:

  - **Scalability**: TensorFlow can run on multiple CPUs or GPUs, making it suitable for large-scale applications.
  - **TensorFlow Serving**: For serving models in production, TensorFlow offers a high-performance, flexible system for serving models with low-latency predictions.
  - **TensorFlow Lite**: This allows the deployment of machine learning models on mobile devices (iOS and Android).
  - **Ecosystem**: TensorFlow supports tools like TensorFlow Hub (for pre-trained models) and TensorFlow Extended (for end-to-end pipelines).

Example Code (Building a Model in TensorFlow/Keras):

```python
import tensorflow as tf
from tensorflow.keras import layers, models

# Define a Sequential model in Keras
model = models.Sequential([
    layers.Dense(64, activation='relu',
input_shape=(784,)),  # Input layer
    layers.Dense(10, activation='softmax')  #
Output layer
])

# Compile the model with optimizer, loss
function, and metrics
model.compile(optimizer='adam',

loss='sparse_categorical_crossentropy',
            metrics=['accuracy'])

# Print model summary
model.summary()
```

- **PyTorch**: PyTorch, developed by Facebook's AI Research lab, is a dynamic computational framework that offers greater flexibility for building neural networks compared to TensorFlow. It's particularly popular in research due to its ease of use, debugging features, and native support for dynamic computational graphs (which makes it more intuitive for certain kinds of experimentation).

Advantages of PyTorch:

- **Dynamic computation graph**: PyTorch uses a dynamic computation graph (also known as "define-by-run"), which allows for more flexibility during model training. It's ideal for situations where the model architecture may change during execution.
- **Debugging**: The dynamic nature makes it easier to debug and experiment with code.
- **Integration with other tools**: PyTorch is highly compatible with other Python libraries such as NumPy, SciPy, and OpenCV, making it easier to use in diverse scenarios.

Example Code (Building a Model in PyTorch):

```python
import torch
import torch.nn as nn
import torch.optim as optim

# Define the network architecture
class SimpleNN(nn.Module):
    def __init__(self):
        super(SimpleNN, self).__init__()
        self.fc1 = nn.Linear(784, 64)  # Fully
connected layer
        self.fc2 = nn.Linear(64, 10)  # Output
layer

    def forward(self, x):
        x = torch.relu(self.fc1(x.view(-1, 784)))
# Flatten the input and apply ReLU
        return self.fc2(x)

model = SimpleNN()
optimizer = optim.Adam(model.parameters(),
lr=0.001)  # Optimizer
criterion = nn.CrossEntropyLoss()  # Loss
function
```

- **Keras**: Keras is a high-level neural network API written in Python that can run on top of TensorFlow. It is designed to be user-friendly, modular, and extensible, which makes it ideal for beginners and rapid prototyping. While TensorFlow provides a low-level API, Keras abstracts many of the details of neural network design, making it easier to get up and running quickly.

  Advantages of Keras:

    o **Simplicity**: Keras abstracts away many complexities, providing an intuitive and user-friendly interface.
    o **Modularity**: You can easily build complex models by stacking pre-built layers.
    o **Integration with TensorFlow**: While Keras is a standalone API, it is tightly integrated with TensorFlow, providing additional functionalities such as TensorFlow's deployment and serving tools.

  Example Code (Building a Model in Keras):

```
from keras.models import Sequential
from keras.layers import Dense

# Initialize the model
model = Sequential()

# Add layers to the model
model.add(Dense(64, activation='relu',
input_shape=(784,)))  # Input layer
model.add(Dense(10, activation='softmax'))  #
Output layer

# Compile the model
model.compile(optimizer='adam',

loss='sparse_categorical_crossentropy',
             metrics=['accuracy'])

# Print model architecture
model.summary()
```

2. Training Models

Training a neural network involves feeding data into the model and updating the model's parameters (weights and biases) based on the error between the predicted and actual outcomes. Let's dive deeper into the training process, including code examples that will help you better understand the flow of data through the model and how to optimize it.

Training with TensorFlow/Keras

In TensorFlow/Keras, the training process is straightforward. After defining the model and compiling it, you can train the model using the `.fit()` method. Here's an example using the MNIST dataset to build a simple image classification model.

```python
import tensorflow as tf
from tensorflow.keras import layers, models
from tensorflow.keras.datasets import mnist
from tensorflow.keras.utils import to_categorical

# Load MNIST dataset
(train_images, train_labels), (test_images,
test_labels) = mnist.load_data()

# Preprocess the data
train_images =
train_images.reshape((train_images.shape[0], 28, 28,
1)).astype('float32') / 255
test_images =
test_images.reshape((test_images.shape[0], 28, 28,
1)).astype('float32') / 255
train_labels = to_categorical(train_labels)
test_labels = to_categorical(test_labels)

# Build a simple CNN model
model = models.Sequential([
    layers.Conv2D(32, (3, 3), activation='relu',
input_shape=(28, 28, 1)),
    layers.MaxPooling2D((2, 2)),
    layers.Flatten(),
    layers.Dense(64, activation='relu'),
    layers.Dense(10, activation='softmax')
])

# Compile the model
model.compile(optimizer='adam',
              loss='categorical_crossentropy',
              metrics=['accuracy'])

# Train the model
model.fit(train_images, train_labels, epochs=5,
batch_size=64, validation_split=0.1)

# Evaluate the model
test_loss, test_acc = model.evaluate(test_images,
test_labels)
print(f'Test accuracy: {test_acc}')
```

Training with PyTorch

In PyTorch, you have more flexibility but also more control over the training loop. The following example shows how to train a simple neural network using PyTorch.

```
import torch
import torch.nn as nn
import torch.optim as optim
from torchvision import datasets, transforms
from torch.utils.data import DataLoader

# Data loading and preprocessing
transform = transforms.Compose([transforms.ToTensor(),
transforms.Normalize((0.5,), (0.5,))])
trainset = datasets.MNIST(root='./data', train=True,
download=True, transform=transform)
trainloader = DataLoader(trainset, batch_size=64,
shuffle=True)

# Model definition
class SimpleNN(nn.Module):
    def __init__(self):
        super(SimpleNN, self).__init__()
        self.fc1 = nn.Linear(784, 64)  # Fully
connected layer
        self.fc2 = nn.Linear(64, 10)  # Output layer

    def forward(self, x):
        x = torch.relu(self.fc1(x.view(-1, 784)))  #
Flatten the input and apply ReLU
        return self.fc2(x)

model = SimpleNN()
optimizer = optim.Adam(model.parameters(), lr=0.001)  #
Optimizer
criterion = nn.CrossEntropyLoss()  # Loss function

# Training loop
for epoch in range(5):
    for images, labels in trainloader:
        optimizer.zero_grad()
```

```
    output = model(images)
    loss = criterion(output, labels)
    loss.backward()  # Backpropagation
    optimizer.step()  # Update weights
print(f"Epoch {epoch+1} completed")
```

3. Optimization and Debugging

Model training often involves fine-tuning hyperparameters, debugging, and adjusting model architecture to improve performance. During training, the model is updated using a backpropagation algorithm, where gradients are computed for each weight and bias in the network. However, training deep neural networks is prone to issues like overfitting, underfitting, or non-convergence. Here's how to optimize and debug your model.

Debugging Training

- **Visualizing Training Progress**: Visualization tools like **TensorBoard** for TensorFlow and **Visdom** for PyTorch can help you track training and validation loss, accuracy, and model weights. Visualizing these metrics during training helps identify potential issues such as overfitting, underfitting, or slow convergence.
- **Gradient Checking**: If the model is not converging or producing bad results, it's essential to check if the gradients are being computed correctly. This can be done through a gradient checking method to ensure there is no bug in the backpropagation algorithm.

Tuning for Performance

- **Hyperparameter Tuning**: Tuning hyperparameters like the learning rate, number of layers, batch size, and activation functions significantly impacts model performance. Techniques like **GridSearchCV** or **RandomizedSearchCV** (in scikit-learn) can be used to automate the search for optimal hyperparameters.
- **Learning Rate Schedulers**: Adjusting the learning rate during training helps prevent oscillations or getting stuck in local minima. A **learning rate scheduler** reduces the learning rate as the number of epochs increases.
- **Regularization**: To prevent overfitting, techniques like **L2 regularization** (weight decay) and **dropout** are widely used. Dropout randomly disables certain neurons during training, forcing the model to learn redundant representations, which helps generalize better on unseen data.

4. Deploying Models

After successful training, the next crucial phase is deploying the trained neural network into production. This involves saving the model, creating an inference pipeline, and setting up an API to allow real-time predictions. Deploying models into real-world applications may involve using cloud services, containerization, and serving models with low-latency.

Moving from Training to Deployment

- **Exporting Models**:
  - **TensorFlow**: You can export trained TensorFlow models into formats such as .h5 or **SavedModel** for deployment.
  - **PyTorch**: PyTorch models are usually saved using torch.save(). Additionally, **TorchScript** can be used for export, which is a serialized representation of the model for efficient deployment.
- **Serving Models**:
  - **TensorFlow Serving**: This is a specialized tool for serving TensorFlow models in production environments. It supports batching requests, version control for models, and multiple deployment options.
  - **Flask API**: A simpler deployment method is creating a REST API with **Flask**, which can handle requests and serve model predictions.

Example of using Flask to deploy a model:

```
from flask import Flask, request, jsonify
import tensorflow as tf

app = Flask(__name__)
model = tf.keras.models.load_model('model.h5')

@app.route('/predict', methods=['POST'])
def predict():
    data = request.get_json()
    prediction = model.predict(data['input'])
    return jsonify({'prediction':
prediction.tolist()})

if __name__ == '__main__':
    app.run(debug=True)
```

Cloud Deployment:

For scalable deployment, **cloud platforms** like **AWS**, **Google Cloud**, and **Microsoft Azure** offer specific services for deploying machine learning models. For example:

- **AWS SageMaker** for training and deploying models at scale.
- **Google AI Platform** for hosting models and running predictions with auto-scaling.
- **Containerization**: Using **Docker** to containerize your model allows it to be packaged with all dependencies, making deployment across different environments seamless. **Kubernetes** can be used to orchestrate the scaling of these containers when handling large-scale predictions.

Future of Neural Networks

- **Recent Advancements**
  - State-of-the-art models and innovations (transformers, GPT-like models).
- **Trends and Future Directions**
  - Quantum computing, neuromorphic computing, AI ethics, etc.

The Future of Neural Networks

The future of neural networks is not just about better models and algorithms but also about an integrated convergence of cutting-edge technologies that will alter how we live, work, and solve global problems. This deep dive will explore advancements, challenges, and potential breakthroughs in the context of neural networks, with a focus on transformative areas such as quantum computing, neuromorphic computing, multi-modal learning, self-learning systems, and ethical considerations.

Technological Innovations and Breakthroughs

1. Quantum Neural Networks (Deep Dive)

Quantum computing is arguably one of the most transformative areas for neural networks. Classical computers are based on binary data processing, but quantum computers use quantum bits or **qubits**, which exist in multiple states simultaneously. This enables the processing of data at an entirely different scale. Neural networks, powered by quantum computing, hold the potential to revolutionize many fields.

- **Superposition and Parallelization**: The power of quantum computing lies in **superposition**, where a qubit can represent both 0 and 1 at the same time. This allows quantum machines to perform multiple calculations at once, potentially exponentially speeding up the training process for large neural networks. Quantum neural networks (QNNs) could leverage this inherent parallelism, making it feasible to solve problems like protein folding, complex simulations, and big-data optimization at previously unimaginable speeds.

- **Quantum-Enhanced Optimization**: One of the key challenges in training deep neural networks is optimization. Classical optimization algorithms, such as gradient descent, can struggle with local minima or inefficiency in complex, high-dimensional spaces. Quantum algorithms, like the **Quantum Approximate Optimization Algorithm (QAOA)**, are being developed to perform optimization tasks more efficiently by leveraging quantum mechanics. This could significantly improve the speed and effectiveness of training deep networks, particularly for high-dimensional data.
- **Quantum Data Representation**: A quantum neural network doesn't just work with classical data—quantum data itself could be used, which means quantum systems could process inherently quantum information. A potential outcome is the ability to model **quantum systems** (such as molecules in quantum chemistry) directly and with much more efficiency compared to classical neural networks.

Real-World Example: Imagine drug discovery where quantum computing could simulate the interaction between molecules in real-time, facilitating rapid testing of potential drug candidates. Neural networks enhanced with quantum computing could revolutionize how pharmaceutical companies approach treatments for diseases.

Neuromorphic computing is rapidly gaining traction because it seeks to emulate the brain's way of processing information. Rather than using a traditional sequential processor, neuromorphic systems use spiking neurons that mimic the way biological neurons interact, giving them an inherent ability to learn and adapt continuously.

- **Spiking Neural Networks (SNNs)**: These networks represent information as a series of discrete events or spikes, closely mimicking the way real neurons operate in the human brain. The **time-based nature** of these spikes allows SNNs to process information asynchronously and efficiently. This could be a major breakthrough for real-time applications, such as decision-making in autonomous systems or real-time video analysis.
- **Energy-Efficient AI**: Neuromorphic chips, designed to simulate how the brain works, use significantly less energy compared to traditional deep learning hardware. This is particularly advantageous for edge AI applications where computational power and energy efficiency are critical. The integration of **low-power neuromorphic chips** with Internet of Things (IoT) devices could lead to breakthroughs in AI for smart homes, health monitoring, and autonomous devices like drones.
- **On-the-Fly Learning**: Neuromorphic networks are capable of **continuous learning** (also called **online learning**), where they can process and learn from data in real time. This is fundamentally different from traditional neural networks, which rely on large datasets and require batch training. In real-world applications like autonomous vehicles or robotics, this ability to continuously adapt to changing environments is a major advantage, leading to more dynamic and responsive systems.

Real-World Example: In robotics, a neuromorphic system could enable a robot to interact with humans naturally by learning from its environment and human feedback. It could adjust its behavior without being explicitly retrained, making it more adaptable in real-time.

3. Multi-Modal Neural Networks (Deep Dive)

The future of AI is in **multi-modal learning**, where neural networks can process multiple forms of data simultaneously—combining images, text, audio, and other forms of sensory input. Multi-modal neural networks are poised to unlock the potential for more **holistic understanding** of the world, allowing machines to learn about various domains in an integrated, human-like way.

- **Unified Models for Different Modalities**: Currently, neural networks tend to be specialized for a single modality (e.g., **Convolutional Neural Networks (CNNs)** for images, **Recurrent Neural Networks (RNNs)** for sequential data). However, multi-modal neural networks are designed to integrate and process different types of data simultaneously. For example, a multi-modal model might be able to interpret an image and a spoken sentence together, making it capable of understanding context and generating captions in real time.
- **Cross-Domain Learning**: Multi-modal learning offers the potential for neural networks to **transfer knowledge** across domains. For example, a neural network trained on visual data could be fine-tuned to interpret speech, enabling systems like autonomous vehicles or robots to learn to integrate visual, auditory, and sensor data in complex environments.

- **Generative Multi-Modal Models**: Multi-modal neural networks can also generate content in multiple modalities. For instance, a **multi-modal GPT-3 model** could take a description in text and generate a realistic image based on that text. This has exciting potential in fields such as entertainment, where AI could assist in generating artwork, video, or music from a simple narrative description.

Real-World Example: A **smart assistant** could integrate vision, sound, and context to better understand its environment and respond more naturally. For example, by recognizing the objects in a room, processing a question about those objects, and responding with both verbal and visual cues (e.g., showing an image), the assistant would have a more human-like conversational ability.

4. Self-Supervised Learning and Autonomous AI (Deep Dive)

Self-supervised learning is poised to transform the way we train neural networks. In self-supervised learning, the system generates labels from raw, unannotated data by predicting parts of the input data. This can significantly reduce the need for labeled datasets, which are often expensive and time-consuming to create.

- **Learning Without Explicit Labels**: Traditional machine learning requires labeled data (e.g., an image labeled with the name of an object). In contrast, self-supervised learning enables models to learn from **raw, unlabeled data**. For instance, models can predict missing parts of an image (e.g., the missing pixels in a partially obscured photo), or predict the next word in a sentence. By doing this, neural networks can learn representations of data, which are then used for downstream tasks like classification or clustering.

- **Improved Efficiency**: Since self-supervised learning doesn't rely on labeled datasets, it enables neural networks to learn from vast amounts of **unlabeled data**, which is far more abundant. This can make AI more accessible to a wider range of fields, from healthcare (where labeled data is often limited) to environmental sciences (where large amounts of sensor data can be leveraged for learning).
- **Autonomous Systems**: Self-supervised learning also has the potential to power **autonomous systems** that can learn directly from interaction with their environments. These systems can continuously improve and adapt based on real-world data rather than being solely dependent on human-provided labels.

Real-World Example: In autonomous driving, a self-supervised neural network could process video footage from cameras in the vehicle to learn about road conditions, vehicle dynamics, and pedestrian behavior without requiring explicitly labeled datasets. Over time, the system becomes more adept at navigating different driving scenarios autonomously.

Ethical Implications and Responsible AI

As neural networks and AI models continue to become more powerful, their ethical implications are drawing significant attention. The intersection of **AI ethics**, **bias** mitigation, and **accountability** will play a critical role in shaping the future landscape of AI.

1. AI and Bias Mitigation (Deep Dive)

AI systems, including neural networks, are highly sensitive to the data they are trained on. **Bias** in training data can lead to biased outcomes, especially in sensitive areas such as hiring, law enforcement, and lending.

- **Bias Detection Tools**: New techniques are being developed to detect and mitigate bias in AI systems. For instance, tools that analyze training data and model outputs for fairness, such as **Fairness Indicators**, can identify disparities across groups and suggest modifications to ensure equitable outcomes.
- **Data Collection and Diversity**: One of the most effective ways to combat bias is through the **diversification** of data. By ensuring that datasets are representative of all demographic groups, researchers can minimize the risk of biased outcomes. In practice, this means ensuring that datasets used for training AI models are not dominated by one group and reflect the diversity of the population it will serve.
- **Explainability and Transparency**: In industries such as healthcare, finance, and criminal justice, the consequences of biased AI decisions can be life-altering. By developing **explainable AI models**, stakeholders can understand the rationale behind a model's decision and ensure that it is not unjustly influenced by biased factors. **Interpretable models** allow users to understand why decisions are made and whether they are aligned with fairness guidelines.

2. AI Regulation and Accountability

With the rise of powerful neural networks and AI models, governance frameworks will be essential to ensure AI is used responsibly.

- **Global Standards for AI Governance**: Governments and international organizations are working on establishing **regulations** to ensure ethical AI use. For example, the European Union's **Artificial Intelligence Act** sets out guidelines for high-risk AI applications, including mandates for transparency, accountability, and human oversight.
- **Human-in-the-Loop (HITL)**: For critical applications such as autonomous weapons, healthcare diagnostics, and criminal justice, ensuring that humans remain in control of decision-making processes is paramount. **HITL** is a key principle that ensures that AI systems make suggestions or provide support, but final decisions are made by humans, especially in areas where moral and legal consequences are involved.
- **Transparency and Auditability**: AI systems, particularly in high-stakes applications, must be subject to

regular audits to ensure they operate as intended. Transparency around how neural networks are trained and how their decisions are made is critical for public trust. Regulatory bodies may require AI companies to maintain logs, document decisions, and provide audit trails.

1. The Technological Evolution

Deepening Architectures and Model Complexity

The next phase of neural networks will likely see even **deeper architectures** with more intricate interconnections. We've already witnessed breakthroughs in the scaling of models such as **GPT-3** and **transformers**, but future advancements are likely to go beyond just increasing the size of these models. Techniques that aim to optimize the structure and operation of neural networks will be central.

- **Smarter Architectures**: We'll see **more specialized neural networks** that integrate hybrid approaches—combining aspects of convolutional networks (CNNs), recurrent networks (RNNs), and transformers. These networks will be tailored to specific tasks, making them more efficient in their respective applications.
- **Neural Architecture Search (NAS)**: The **automatic design of neural network architectures** using AI will continue to evolve, leading to novel network designs that we might not have previously thought of. These networks will be optimized for specific use cases, potentially improving the performance and reducing the computational cost of training large-scale models.

Integration with Quantum Computing and Neuromorphic Computing

The fusion of neural networks with emerging technologies, particularly **quantum computing** and **neuromorphic computing**, is expected to bring about the next wave of breakthroughs.

- **Quantum Computing**: As mentioned earlier, quantum computing can vastly accelerate neural network computations, particularly in high-dimensional spaces that classical computers struggle with. The coupling of quantum algorithms with deep learning models will enable the tackling of some of the most complex computational tasks, such as simulating molecular structures for drug discovery or solving optimization problems in large-scale operations.
- **Neuromorphic Computing**: Neuromorphic computing, inspired by the structure and function of the brain, promises to radically change how we implement neural networks. The potential for ultra-low-power, real-time learning systems means that applications in robotics, autonomous systems, and even smart environments will become more practical and efficient.

2. AI in Real-World Applications: The Transformation of Industries

The landscape of **AI applications** will continue to evolve, extending into new areas where neural networks will play an increasingly central role. These applications will revolutionize industries, reshape existing business models, and enable entirely new domains of innovation.

Healthcare and Life Sciences

In healthcare, **neural networks** and AI are on the verge of radically transforming everything from diagnosis to personalized treatment.

- **AI-Powered Diagnostics**: Deep learning models have already demonstrated their ability to identify diseases like cancer, heart conditions, and neurological disorders with incredible precision. In the future, we can expect even more advanced diagnostic systems that rely on AI to not only detect disease but predict the progression and response to treatments. These systems will be integrated with medical imaging, genomics, and even wearable health technologies.
- **Drug Discovery and Genomic Research**: Neural networks will continue to assist in drug discovery by predicting the interactions between proteins, molecules, and drug compounds. **AI-driven precision medicine**—where treatments are tailored to an individual's genetic makeup—will become more widespread, potentially leading to significant improvements in patient outcomes.

Autonomous Systems and Robotics

Neural networks are already at the heart of many autonomous systems. In the near future, we'll witness their deployment in a variety of sectors, with profound implications for industries such as transportation, manufacturing, and logistics.

- **Self-Driving Cars**: While autonomous vehicles are still in the testing and development stages, deep learning models, particularly those designed for **computer vision** and **sensor fusion**, will continue to advance. The neural networks behind self-driving cars will become smarter, capable of handling more complex scenarios and dealing with edge cases that involve unexpected interactions in real-world traffic conditions.
- **Smart Robotics**: The ability of robots to understand their environment and interact with humans will be increasingly enhanced by neural networks. Robotics powered by AI will likely improve efficiency and safety in industries like manufacturing, healthcare (surgical robots, assistive robots for the elderly), and hazardous environments (e.g., deep-sea exploration, disaster recovery).

Artificial Intelligence in Creative Domains

The creative industries will also experience a significant transformation as AI and neural networks enhance how art, music, design, and entertainment are produced.

- **Generative AI**: Neural networks are already creating art, music, and even literature. As **Generative Adversarial Networks (GANs)** and transformers evolve, we'll likely see **AI-generated content** become more indistinguishable from human-created works. This could impact everything from video game design to content generation for marketing, with AI potentially creating personalized media tailored to individual tastes and preferences.
- **Personalized Content**: With the help of neural networks, platforms like streaming services, e-commerce websites, and social media will provide more personalized experiences based on individual preferences. By analyzing vast amounts of data, AI will offer increasingly tailored recommendations in real-time.

3. Ethical Considerations and Responsible AI

As neural networks grow in sophistication, their ethical implications are becoming a central focus. AI systems will have to be designed not only for performance but also with a strong emphasis on fairness, accountability, and transparency.

Addressing Bias and Fairness

AI systems are only as good as the data they are trained on, and datasets that reflect societal biases can lead to biased models. In the future, **bias mitigation** will become a core part of neural network development.

- **Fairness Algorithms**: We can expect the development of better **bias detection** and **bias correction techniques**, making AI models fairer and more equitable. This will be especially important in applications like hiring, lending, and criminal justice, where biased decisions can have severe real-world consequences.
- **Diverse Datasets**: Moving forward, researchers will place more emphasis on curating datasets that represent **diverse** populations and scenarios. AI models trained on diverse, well-represented data will help prevent skewed or discriminatory outcomes.

Transparency and Explainability

One of the most pressing challenges facing neural networks is their **black-box** nature—where decisions made by AI systems are difficult for humans to interpret.

- **Explainable AI (XAI)**: As neural networks become more integrated into decision-making processes, particularly in high-stakes areas like healthcare and finance, the need for **transparent AI** will intensify. Researchers are already working on methods to make AI decisions more interpretable. For example, **local interpretable models** like LIME and SHAP are helping provide insights into how deep learning models reach their conclusions.
- **Accountability**: There will be growing demands for AI systems to be accountable for their decisions. Regulators and businesses alike will need to implement mechanisms to ensure that AI systems are not only high-performing but also fair, just, and understandable to humans.

As AI systems become more embedded in daily life, **privacy** concerns will continue to rise.

- **Federated Learning**: One potential solution to data privacy issues is **federated learning**, which allows models to train on local devices rather than centralized servers, ensuring that user data stays private. This technique can be especially important for **healthcare** applications, where data privacy is critical.
- **Data Sovereignty**: In the future, governments and international organizations may implement stricter laws governing the use and sharing of personal data. The landscape of AI will need to balance innovation with **user consent** and **data sovereignty** to respect individuals' privacy rights.

4. The Path Forward: Embracing Collaboration and Interdisciplinary Research

Looking ahead, it's clear that neural networks and AI will not evolve in isolation. The **future of AI** will be shaped by a collaboration between diverse disciplines, including:

- **Ethicists and Social Scientists**: To ensure that AI technologies are developed responsibly, ethicists and social scientists must work alongside data scientists and engineers to navigate the social implications of AI.
- **Cross-Industry Partnerships**: The rapid pace of AI research will be driven by partnerships between academic institutions, tech companies, startups, and government agencies. Collaborative research and shared innovation will accelerate progress in neural network technology and its applications.

- **Education and Workforce Development**: As AI becomes increasingly pervasive, there will be an increasing need for **AI literacy** across all sectors. This means that educational programs must evolve to equip students with the skills to both build and use AI systems. Likewise, the workforce will need reskilling to adapt to new jobs created by AI technologies.

Final Thoughts: A Transformative Future for Neural Networks

The road ahead for neural networks is one of incredible promise. From transforming industries to enhancing our everyday lives, the potential applications are vast. Yet, as these technologies evolve, there is a pressing need to ensure they are developed responsibly, ethically, and inclusively.

As we continue to innovate, the challenge will not just be to develop more powerful, accurate, and efficient neural networks, but to do so in a way that benefits all of humanity. The next generation of AI will undoubtedly bring about new possibilities, but it is up to us to guide its development in a way that promotes fairness, transparency, and the betterment of society.

The evolving landscape of neural networks and AI is not just about technological achievement, but also about shaping a future where AI serves humanity's best interests—creating a world that is smarter, more connected, and more responsible.

References and Learn More Options About Artificial Neural Networks

For students interested in diving deeper into Artificial Neural Networks (ANNs), understanding both the theoretical foundations and practical implementations is crucial. Below are a variety of references, resources, and tips to guide learning, along with a bibliography and appendix for further study.

1. Core Books on Artificial Neural Networks

- **"Neural Networks and Deep Learning: A Textbook" by Charu Aggarwal**
  This book provides an in-depth introduction to neural networks, offering both theoretical concepts and practical techniques for understanding deep learning and ANN architectures. It's an excellent resource for both students and professionals.
- **"Deep Learning" by Ian Goodfellow, Yoshua Bengio, and Aaron Courville**
  Often regarded as the most authoritative text on deep learning, this book covers everything from basic neural network theory to advanced deep learning techniques, making it an essential read for anyone serious about the field.
- **"Pattern Recognition and Machine Learning" by Christopher M. Bishop**
  This book offers a solid foundation in machine learning and pattern recognition, with a detailed explanation of neural networks and their mathematical foundations. It's ideal for those looking to understand the statistical underpinnings of machine learning and neural networks.

- **"Neural Networks for Pattern Recognition" by Christopher Bishop**
  A foundational work that focuses specifically on pattern recognition with neural networks, this book is a valuable resource for understanding how ANNs can be applied to classification and pattern recognition tasks.

2. Online Courses and Tutorials

- **Coursera - "Deep Learning Specialization" by Andrew Ng**
  This specialization consists of five courses, covering everything from neural networks and backpropagation to more advanced deep learning architectures. It's an excellent hands-on course that gives students practical exposure to ANN concepts.
- **Fast.ai - "Practical Deep Learning for Coders"**
  Fast.ai offers a very hands-on course that emphasizes real-world applications. The course uses the Fastai library and PyTorch, making it great for learners who want to dive straight into coding deep learning models.
- **Udacity - "Intro to TensorFlow for Deep Learning"**
  A course by Udacity that focuses on how to use TensorFlow (a popular machine learning framework) to build deep learning models. It's ideal for beginners who want to quickly start implementing neural networks in Python.
- **Stanford University - CS231n: Convolutional Neural Networks for Visual Recognition**
  A more advanced course that delves into convolutional neural networks (CNNs), ideal for students who are specifically interested in computer vision and the applications of neural networks in image processing.

3. Research Papers and Journals

- **Journal of Machine Learning Research (JMLR)**
  JMLR is a peer-reviewed journal that publishes cutting-edge research in machine learning, including deep learning and neural networks. It's a great resource for students looking to explore current research trends in the field.
- **"Backpropagation Through Time: What It Does and How to Do It" by Paul J. Werbos (1990)**
  This paper introduced backpropagation through time (BPTT), a key algorithm for training recurrent neural networks (RNNs). It's a foundational paper for understanding the history and mechanics of deep learning.
- **"ImageNet Classification with Deep Convolutional Neural Networks" by Alex Krizhevsky, Ilya Sutskever, and Geoffrey Hinton (2012)**
  This landmark paper describes the deep convolutional neural network (CNN) that won the ImageNet competition, revolutionizing the field of computer vision. It's a must-read for understanding the power of deep learning.
- **ArXiv Preprints**
  ArXiv.org is a repository of preprints for research papers in various fields, including machine learning and neural networks. Many groundbreaking research papers in deep learning appear on ArXiv before being published in journals. Students can follow the latest developments by checking out the **Machine Learning** section on ArXiv.

4. Frameworks and Tools

- **TensorFlow**
  TensorFlow, developed by Google, is one of the most widely used machine learning frameworks. It's particularly known for its ability to deploy deep learning models on various platforms. Students should familiarize themselves with TensorFlow's extensive documentation and tutorials.
- **PyTorch**
  PyTorch is another popular deep learning framework, known for its dynamic computational graph and simplicity of use. It has become increasingly favored for research and is widely used in academia. PyTorch's official tutorials provide a great hands-on introduction to neural networks.
- **Keras**
  Keras is a high-level API built on top of TensorFlow and Theano, offering a simple and user-friendly way to define neural networks. It's great for beginners and offers extensive documentation and examples.
- **Scikit-learn**
  While Scikit-learn is not focused on deep learning, it provides several essential machine learning algorithms, including basic neural networks. It's a good starting point for students to learn about machine learning before diving into deep learning frameworks.

5. Tips and Tricks for Students

- **Understand the Basics**: Before jumping into coding neural networks, ensure you have a strong understanding of the underlying mathematics, particularly linear algebra, calculus, and probability. These areas are fundamental to understanding how neural networks work.
- **Start Small**: Begin with small-scale models like single-layer perceptrons (SLPs) or simple feedforward neural networks.

Build up to more complex architectures like CNNs or RNNs as you grow more comfortable.

- **Practice Regularly**: Deep learning is a hands-on field. Regularly work on coding exercises, such as implementing simple neural networks from scratch or using frameworks like TensorFlow or PyTorch.
- **Experiment with Datasets**: Work with real-world datasets (e.g., MNIST, CIFAR-10, or even Kaggle datasets) to practice building and tuning your models. Experiment with different architectures, learning rates, and hyperparameters to understand their effects.
- **Read Research Papers**: Try reading at least one recent research paper a week related to neural networks or deep learning. This will help you stay current with innovations and understand the theoretical aspects that drive practical applications.
- **Join Communities**: Participate in AI and machine learning communities, such as StackOverflow, Reddit's /r/MachineLearning, or AI conferences like NeurIPS. Engaging with others will help you solve problems, find new resources, and stay inspired.
- **Use Pretrained Models**: When starting with complex tasks (like natural language processing or computer vision), leverage pretrained models. They can save time and provide high-performance benchmarks that you can fine-tune for specific applications.

- **Monitor the Evolution of the Field**: AI is rapidly evolving, so stay curious and up to date with the latest advancements. Subscribe to newsletters, follow thought leaders on Twitter, and keep an eye on conferences to see where the field is heading.

Bibliography

- Aggarwal, Charu. **Neural Networks and Deep Learning: A Textbook**. Springer, 2018.
- Goodfellow, Ian, Yoshua Bengio, and Aaron Courville. **Deep Learning**. MIT Press, 2016.
- Bishop, Christopher M. **Pattern Recognition and Machine Learning**. Springer, 2006.
- Werbos, Paul J. "Backpropagation Through Time: What It Does and How to Do It." *Proceedings of the IEEE*, 1990.
- Krizhevsky, Alex, Ilya Sutskever, and Geoffrey Hinton. "ImageNet Classification with Deep Convolutional Neural Networks." *Neural Information Processing Systems (NIPS)*, 2012.

Appendix

A. Neural Network Terminology

- **Neuron**: A computational unit that processes input data.
- **Weight**: A parameter that adjusts the importance of each input in a neural network.
- **Bias**: A constant value added to the input of a neuron to shift the output, helping the model learn better.
- **Activation Function**: A mathematical function applied to the output of each neuron, such as Sigmoid, ReLU, or Tanh.
- **Backpropagation**: A training algorithm that adjusts weights and biases by propagating errors backward through the network.

B. Example Neural Network Code Snippet (using Keras)

```
import keras
from keras.models import Sequential
from keras.layers import Dense
import numpy as np

# Generating some simple data
X = np.array([[0, 0], [0, 1], [1, 0], [1, 1]])  # Input data
y = np.array([[0], [1], [1], [0]])  # XOR labels

# Creating a simple feedforward neural network model
model = Sequential()
model.add(Dense(10, input_dim=2, activation='relu'))  # Hidden layer
model.add(Dense(1, activation='sigmoid'))  # Output layer

# Compile the model
model.compile(loss='binary_crossentropy', optimizer='adam', metrics=['accuracy'])

# Train the model
model.fit(X, y, epochs=1000, verbose=0)

# Evaluate the model
loss, accuracy = model.evaluate(X, y)
print(f'Loss: {loss}, Accuracy: {accuracy}')
```

This simple neural network is designed to learn the XOR operation, providing a starting point for students interested in experimenting with neural networks.

----------0o0---------

www.ingramcontent.com/pod-product-compliance
Lightning Source LLC
LaVergne TN
LVHW022349060326
832902LV00022B/4331